THE STRUCTURE OF
HORACE'S ODES

UNIVERSITY OF DURHAM
PUBLICATIONS

THE STRUCTURE OF
HORACE'S ODES

BY

N. E. COLLINGE

*Senior Lecturer in Classics
in the Durham Colleges
in the University of Durham*

LONDON
OXFORD UNIVERSITY PRESS
NEW YORK TORONTO
1961

Oxford University Press, Amen House, London E.C.4

GLASGOW NEW YORK TORONTO MELBOURNE WELLINGTON
BOMBAY CALCUTTA MADRAS KARACHI KUALA LUMPUR
CAPE TOWN IBADAN NAIROBI ACCRA

PRINTED IN GREAT BRITAIN

TO
MILDRED COLLINGE

PREFACE

THE appearance of another book on Horace needs no apology. Undying interest, and the constant spilling of ink, is the price the poet pays for having caught the world's imagination with his words, especially his lyric words. And this imagination has not altered so much, even yet, that we must look for new judgements on the Odes. But to move towards this poetry by fresh approaches and to reach new ground even for forming old judgements—this is something we owe, to Horace in part, to ourselves much more. The major task, after all, is to refine our own sensitivity and to open our own eyes a little wider. For one thing, enthusiasm is no longer enough: one who calls attention to 'this sublime poem', or opines that 'Horace here achieves perfection', and offers no word of how or why, no general theory of poetry's nature and of Horatian composition, is merely obscurantist. Not that such general theorizing is entirely absent from the existing treatments, although classical scholars complacently allow poets, students of other literatures, and civil servants to make much of the running on this road. But the thing is patchily done; and perhaps the greatest desiderata are something more than a mere classification of Horace's metaphors according to their content, and something beyond the usual *ad hoc* solutions of the transitions of his lyric thought. Recent years have seen more and more scholarly detective work on Horace's sources of inspiration, on those who said Horatian things before he did: yet the most erudite literary genealogies will not help us to evaluate Horace as a craftsman unless we have already studied the mechanics of each of his poems. We could deny him any craftsmanship at all in a poem if we had its 'original' before us entire and found it to differ in no particular, in sense, length, structure, and emphasis, from Horace's version: in no case is this so.

Therefore, if no apology, at least a word of explanation for this present study: that it is an attempt to find sense—and beauty—in the *design* of the Odes. Its preconception is that the same general theory of formal analysis may with profit be applied to the words which convey Horace's thoughts, to the thoughts which make his poems, and even to the whole poems which build his lyric corpus. And comfort may be drawn from the fact that nobody could be more self-conscious and fastidious a composer than Horace himself, nobody less tolerant of the *occupet extremum scabies* school. The Odes, too, are very largely exercises in form, to the exclusion of content, or at least to the exclusion of fresh invention. This the reader may test by working out for himself how many odes, of quite different design, are built from the mere ideas contained in, say, *Epodes* xiii and xv alone. It does not do, therefore, for the Horatian critic to be too nice in distinguishing 'intrinsic' from 'constructional' values.

We must re-read Horace, with attention. If we have a clearer understanding of what he has done in the Odes, we shall be the more able to decide whether to love him or hate him for doing it. Besides, with a little more light shed on matters of construction, facile (and false) comparisons and excessive emphasis on favourite passages may become less fashionable in criticism. To these ends it is hoped this survey will lead: but it needs one essential concomitant—a text of the Odes open at the reader's side. This will not only let him see, in context, the words of the poet which are under debate, and so judge whether this book is talking sense (or will perhaps lead others to a position where sense might be talked); it will also permit him a synoptic view of the ode in question, and only so can he appreciate in this discussion those physical relationships of space, of placing, and of proportion which play no small part.

My grateful thanks are due to the Council of the Durham Colleges for the sabbatical leave which enabled me to begin the manuscript, and for financial help towards its typing; to the Publications Board of the University of Durham for accepting the work within its series; and to the chairman of that Board, Professor H. S. Offler, for his unfailing kindness and skill in steering me through the administrative intricacies which beset an author. I have also appreciated the help of Dr. W. E. Saxton in seeing the book through the press.

As to the subject-matter, I have discussed details with few but generalities with many; for, to my delight, I have not found a scholar who will not talk readily and warmly about Horace. I learned very much from the conversations and correspondence of the late Professor A. Y. Campbell; my debts to others, on particular points, are acknowledged in the footnotes. But it is Mr. L. P. Wilkinson who, above all, deserves my gratitude. Not only did he read the work in an early draft and make many acute and helpful observations on it, but at a later date came literally out of his way to read it with me again, pointing to errors, castigating obscurities, and widening references. Faults remain: those who find them must impute them to me alone.

N. E. C.

Durham
March 1960

CONTENTS

SELECT LIST OF ABBREVIATIONS

AJP	*American Journal of Philology.*
Athen.	*Athenaeum.*
BICS	*Bulletin of the Institute of Classical Studies.*
Bursians Jb.	*Bursians Jahresberichte über die Fortschritte der klassischen Altertumswissenschaft.*
CJ	*Classical Journal.*
CP	*Classical Philology.*
CQ	*Classical Quarterly.*
CR	*Classical Review.*
CW	*Classical Weekly* (now *Classical World*).
Ét. Class.	*Études Classiques.*
JHS	*Journal of Hellenic Studies.*
JRS	*Journal of Roman Studies.*
LSJ	*Greek–English Lexicon* by Liddell and Scott, ninth edition by Stuart Jones and McKenzie.
Mus. Helv.	*Museum Helveticum.*
Rh. Mus.	*Rheinisches Museum für Philologie.*
TAPA	*Transactions of the American Philological Association.*

The names of journals other than the above are given in full. Where journals repaginate annually, reference is made by means of year and page only (series and volume numbers being otiose).

Two recent works are so often quoted as to make it convenient to use the author's name alone, followed by the page reference. They are:

Fraenkel   E. Fraenkel, *Horace*, O.U.P. 1957.

Wilkinson   L. P. Wilkinson, *Horace and his Lyric Poetry*², C.U.P. 1951.

For Horace's own works, the abbreviations used are: *AP*, 'Ars Poetica' (*ad Pisones*); *C*, *Carmina* (Odes); *Carm. Saec.*, *Carmen Saeculare*; *Epi.*, Epistles; *Epo.*, Epodes; *S*, *Sermones* (Satires).

I

Words and Images: The Mechanistic Approach

Operosa carmina sound depressing. Yet the labour of the file has won Horace the delighted approval of so many readers for so many years as almost to have exorcized the deep-seated preconception that poetry (and especially lyric poetry) is an ethereal and spontaneous phenomenon. In fact, lyric poetry too has its 'makers' and 'builders' who are not to be written off, from the critical point of view, as ἔνθεοι and ἔκφρονες, abiding our question not at all. They themselves tell us much on the contrary, directly and indirectly, of the toil and sweat, the doing and undoing, and the workings of that sad process by which (as Shelley says) 'when composition begins, inspiration is already on the decline; and the most glorious poetry that has ever been communicated to the world is probably a feeble shadow of the original conceptions of the poet'. If in our hearts we are slow to believe this, then the study of any ancient lyricist is a salutary experience (the quantitative metre alone argues a mental discipline of more than common strictness); to study Horace—and the mountains of comparative and interpretative exegesis which his Odes alone have occasioned— is particularly illuminating. Commentators have written but sporadically on the structural aspects of the Odes, and then mostly at the level of word and phrase, with italics and underlinings and adroit capitals pointing the relationships they would have us ponder: to add to this cumulation would win small thanks. But at this level the implications of 'felicitas' have been stressed to the exclusion of the implications of 'curiosa', so to put it: there has been more concern with products than with processes : and critics (especially textual critics, who incline as a class to the optimistic) have seemed ready to believe that what is carefully composed must be perfectly composed, and (a subtler error) that this perfection consists of the fullest possible exploitation of every ounce of significance which a word or phrase, by position as well as intrinsically, can convey. Nietzsche was in the van of this approach, with his commendation of the Odes as 'this mosaic of words, in which every word by sound, by position, and by meaning diffuses its influence to right and left and over the whole'.[1] Of course, in a mosaic every piece has its place and its function, and it is the function of some to be neutral. But Nietzsche has been understood to mean that every word carries full colour. Such a policy (to change the figure) would be a rich cake indeed; fortunately for our aesthetic digestions Horace really offers fare more varied and less cloying.

It is easy to satisfy oneself of this. In the choice of words alone, for every new use Horace offers a conventional one, for every bold venture a tame, safe combination, for every breath-taking aptness a frigid failure. And this is a decided merit, taken as a whole. We can temper the full relish of 'splendide mendax' or 'auritas quercus' or 'gravis principum amicitias' with the insipidity of 'prata canis albicant pruinis', 'pomifer autumnus', or 'manus avidas heredis', and so preserve our perceptiveness of taste in readiness for the delicate savour of 'placens uxor', 'Hannibalem dirum', 'raptor inaudax', and a dozen such *proprie* (*nec nimis*) *dicta*. New-minted coin like 'vultus lubricus' or 'ingeni vena' or the curious 'diem mero fregi' jingle alongside more worn (if well-designed) currency— as 'maculosum nefas' recalls Cicero's 'maculosi senatores', as

---

[1] From 'Was ich den Alten verdanke', *Götzendämmerung* (1888), 175 ff. This is Wilkinson's version (4): and this is the line of thought which flowers, for instance, in his own valuable fifth chapter (123 ff.) on 'the Horatian Ode'. This type of analysis goes hand in hand with *Lautmalerei* studies ('artiste de sons' is a typical title; and cf. the group of studies by J. Marouzeau, listed by Burck, Kiessling–Heinze, i⁸. 604): both are taken to excess in H. Hommel's recent *Horaz* (1950). (I prefer, with my italics, A. Y. Campbell's remark: 'in an ode of Horace *almost* every *other* word has a structural function'—edn.² (1953), ix.)

'derivata clades' picks up not only Cicero's but Terence's and Lucretius' usage, as 'columen rerum' or 'stantem columnam' reminds the reader of Plautus' 'senati columen' or Terence's 'columen familiae'—or even as 'lene tormentum' turns out to be but a new dress for Bacchylides' γλυκεῖ᾿ ἀνάγκα.[1] In a similar fashion operates the interplay between vacuous adjectival usage and its strictly meaningful counterpart. It is not simply, however, that the purely expletive '*beatis* gazis' or '*amoenae* rosae' (or, to try one's patience, '*missilibus* sagittis')[2] are offset by hard-working epithets like 'tenuis' or 'sollicitus', which carry with them in all their contexts Horace's philosophy of modest desires and his pity for the man of affairs and of politics. It is rather that sometimes practically no adjective is dispensable while elsewhere many an epithet could disappear without detriment. On the one hand, in the twenty-four verses of the ode to Licinius (ii. 10) perhaps only 'iniquum' in *v.* 4 and 'informis' in *v.* 15 could be removed without loss of basic sense; similarly in i. 18. 14–16, the meaning is simply not accessible through the personified nouns alone but depends on the descriptive phrases and their near-paradoxes:

> *caecus* Amor *sui*
> et *tollens vacuum plus nimio* Gloria *verticem*
> *arcanique* Fides *prodiga.*

But when Hannibal's speech forms the climax of the Drusus-ode (iv. 4. 49–68), little is effected by 'perfidus', 'rapacium', 'maturos', 'duris', 'nigrae' (for the contrast of i. 21. 6–8 is not here exploited), 'Echioniae', 'multa': all these might drop out and leave the essential meaning clear. In this respect there is considerable interweaving to produce a satisfactory texture:

---

[1] iv. 5. 22 and Cic. *Att.* i. 16. 3; iii. 6. 19 and Ter. *Phorm.* 323, Lucr. ii. 365, Cic. *Mil.* 10. 29; ii. 17. 4, i. 35. 14 and Plaut. *Cas.* 536, Ter. *Phorm.* 287 (and see Fraenkel, 217 n. 2); iii. 21. 13 and Bacchyl. fr. 20 B Snell, *v.* 6. And many more: the toil is to discover unprecedented locutions. Puzzle: which was written first—ii. 9. 22 or Virg. *Aen.* viii. 726?

[2] Vacuous epithets are not uncommonly inserted for stylistic balance alone: cf. *honestae* (ii. 18. 8); *liquidum* (ii. 20. 2); and the quite superfluous *impia* of iii. 1. 17.

in this very section of the Drusus-ode it is worth musing, by contrast, on the essential information signalled by 'cremato', 'Tuscis' and 'Ausonias', 'secto', 'integrum'. In the two final stanzas, where the focus is suddenly sharpened, nothing except the repeated *occidit* needs a stylistic defence.

It may be argued that this is simply inconsistency, or at any rate that mere difference is being dignified with the title of 'contrast' or *variatio*. But that Horace is alive to the textural possibilities of contrast is very clear, if only from hints like

'*certus* enim promisit Apollo
ambiguam tellure nova Salamina futuram'
(i. 7. 28 f.)

or

quid mirum, ubi illis carminibus *stupens*
demittit atras belua centiceps
auris et intorti capillis
Eumenidum *recreantur* angues?
(ii. 13. 33 ff.)

or

qui *siccis* oculis monstra *natantia*
. . . vidit
(i. 3. 18 f.)

or, most succinctly,

te per aquas, *dure, volubilis*.
(iv. 1. 40)

It will not be surprising if more extensive and more complex structures present themselves in these poems: and in fact words and phrases (and images) seem to have three kinds of relational functions: (*a*) expressing, more or less overtly, the relationship between whole odes—hence cross-quotation, reminiscence of phraseology from ode to ode, or effects like the *aditure mecum . . . mecum deducte* of ii. 6 and 7; (*b*) conveying the structural 'punctuation' inside individual odes;[1] and (*c*) offering, within their own restricted section of the total utterance, apprehensible patterns of their own, which may be allied to

[1] On uses (*a*) and (*b*) see below, Chaps. II and III.

but are quite separate from their descriptive and emotive contribution.

The last of these functions concerns us for the moment. An
example of it may serve as a guide to what can be achieved at
other levels; and the third stanza of the ode to Dellius (ii. 3.
9–12) affords a fine instance:

> quo pinus ingens albaque populus
> umbram hospitalem consociare amant
> ramis? quid obliquo laborat
> lympha fugax trepidare rivo?

At least three antitheses are employed to create this picture.
First, there is that between the trees themselves, the dark pine
and the light-leaved poplar, the former spreading itself where
the latter rises slender to its top;[1] secondly, the picture is
articulated by the vertical lines which carry the eye up to the
overarching foliage and are in turn offset by the low horizontal
sweep of the brush which paints in the stream across our line of
sight (and so *obliquo rivo*);[2] and lastly, the dignity and silence
and stillness of the branches are answered by the excited and

---

[1] *Ingens albaque* operates in the fashion of double-comparison peculiar to
Horace; so in iii. 13. 6 f. *nam gelidos inficiet tibi rubro sanguine rivos*, where the
water is cold *and silver*, the blood red *and warm* (similarly *veros timores* at i. 37. 15
imply the contrasting 'vanae spes'). But it is easier to be certain of this than of
the precise terms of contrast in ii. 3. What does *pinus ingens* mean? Perhaps
height is the point, for there is no need for the trees to be at all equal in that
respect: Horace does not say, as many commentators do, that they entwine
their branches, but only that they produce a joint shade. Moreover *ingens pinus*
at ii. 10. 9 f. cannot refer to anything but the loftiness of the tree (cf. *celsae
turres, summos montis*). But pine and poplar are not clearly so distinct: some
poplars are taller than some pines in individual cases, and the poplar has
always a high 'aspect-ratio', so to put it, and looks tall. 'Bulky pine' is perhaps
safe (despite ii. 10), and I am grateful to Professor W. B. Stanford for suggesting
it to me. (Miss Toll seems to have a similar explanation in *Phoenix*, 1955, 157:
her contrast words are 'huge' and 'slender'.)

[2] See *CR*, 1949, 7 f.; 1950, 12 f. Despite these essays it is safer to accept the
simple implications of, for example, Lucan i. 220 (*primus in obliquum sonipes
opponitur amnem*): A is *obliquus* to B if the mean forward motion of A is at roughly
90° to that of B. Here A is the stream: B is either the vertical axis of the trees
or our line of sight towards the canvas, so to speak. The mountain-side in Val.
Flacc. i. 484 (*per obliqui rapidum compendia montis*) is practically, allowing for
poetic exaggeration, at 90° to the level shore, and Acastus is coming straight
down it in his haste, as *compendia* (= ἀτραπός) shows.

hardworking currents of the ever-moving rivulet. So, in i. 4, do Venus and the Nymphs and Graces partner Vulcan and his Cyclopes, or the dark myrtle the fresh spring flowers (and in *seu poscat agna sive malit haedo* not merely the unexpressed contrast of the respective submissiveness and skittishness of these victims is pointed, but so is the gender- and sound-variation of male and female).[1] And in the second part of this ode[2] 'pauperum tabernas' and 'regum turris', 'brevis' and 'longam', 'iuventus' and 'virgines' act as conjoined and balancing elements in the poem's building. The thought-structure of iii. 6 (*Delicta maiorum immeritus lues*) affords a symmetrical interplay between *vv.* 21–32 and 33–44, but the terms of description have their own closely-knit scheme of verbal antitheses: one may note, within *vv.* 25–32 (of successive stages of the profligate wife's degeneration):

eligit . . . *but then* iussa surgit . . .
cui donet gaudia . . . *but then* dedecorum pretiosus emptor . . .
raptim . . . luminibus remotis . . . *but then* coram . . .
impermissa gaudia . . . *but then* non sine conscio marito.[3]

The compositional method of 'our antithetic bard', as A. Y. Campbell calls him, seems therefore to be very much a matter of exploiting the combined force of expressional elements which are balanced or contrasted in themselves: and this contrast and combination may operate within a short space or over a considerable distance between odes in the collection (for it is essential to the appreciation of this corpus to regard it as just that—a body of many members set in a certain spatial

---

[1] Cf. *Epo.* xi. 27 f.; *S* ii. 3. 325; *C* i. 27. 11 f. (here neuter–feminine).

[2] For the parts and the verbal linkage, see pp. 95 ff. It is not easy to decide if such internal balances are best dealt with as patterns of words, of imagery (cf. Tracy on the parts of i. 9, *Greece and Rome*, 1948, 105), or of 'atmosphere'. No such subtle distinctions are attempted in Chap. III.

[3] If the matter is reduced to its simplest feature, which is the mere choice of words to convey basic items of sense where no exigencies of thought-movement control the form of expression, then the impulse is clearly and naturally towards partial or full variation: so *semper . . . usque . . . mensis per omnis . . . semper . . . omnis annos . . . semper* in ii. 9, or *pelago . . . freta . . . mare . . . Oceano . . . vada* in i. 3, or *pretium . . . aurum . . . lucrum . . , munera . . . pecuniam* in iii. 16.

relation each to each). Even the mere speed of expression or description may be set in contrastive relationship (as when Pindar in his Argonaut-story turns aside from the slow progress of the high road of narrative and saves time by his celebrated short cut[1]) : nothing could be more economical than the four verses at the centre of the *laudes Mercuri* (i. 10. 9–12)[2] which give practically the entire plot of the fourth Homeric Hymn or Sophocles' *Ichneutae*; but the force of their terseness is redoubled by comparison with the leisurely narration of the Regulus-story in iii. 5 or Europe's adventures in iii. 27. At one moment Horace will hold us open-mouthed for several verses merely to turn the screw of tension (as in i. 22. 9–12 or iii. 4. 9–13) ;[3] at another, in equal compass he will carry us headlong through a year's natural events, or through four generations of morally declining mankind (iv. 7. 9–12; iii. 6. 46–48) : and these extremes themselves derive their power from contrast with the normal velocity of the verse.

These are mere preliminaries : as much might be said of the words of any poet. But it is worth while saying it of Horace—the Horace of the Odes—for he tends to be assigned an inscrutable perfection and super-economy of verbiage; and this only hinders appreciation. It is no doubt in his *imagery*, however, that a poet's individuality of expression (or expressiveness) can best be measured. The question will at once suggest itself : should it not be first established that the imagery of the particular poet we are considering does really deserve to be examined under the heading of verbal expression rather than under that of thought and thought-structure? Let us not seem to beg this question : but it may be instructive to notice how mechanistic is the way in which Horace's pattern-making zeal exploits this further simple contrast, that between plain and figurative language. Amid the adulatory plaudits of iv. 5 (*Divis orte bonis*) come eight verses which, one by one, pronounce the

---

[1] *Pyth.* iv. 247 f. Ten verses complete the story of Jason and tell as much of action as the previous two hundred. (Aeschylus 'blows up' into two plays what Pindar quite reasonably puts into one and a half verses at *Pyth.* xi. 36 f.)

[2] See Fraenkel, 162–5.   [3] See p. 80.

virtues of the *pax Augusta* in a metronomic, one might say a hypnotic, manner:

> tutus bos etenim rura perambulat;   17
> nutrit rura Ceres almaque Faustitas;
> pacatum volitant per mare navitae;
> culpari metuit Fides;
>
> nullis polluitur casta domus stupris;   21
> Mos et Lex maculosum edomuit Nefas;
> laudantur simili prole puerperae;
> Culpam Poena premit comes.

Certainly there is much here that, if the text is sound, is repetitive, even otiose, in thought and in word (*rura . . . rura, culpari . . . Culpam*, etc.); *v.* 17 is pedestrian in two senses, while *v.* 23 seems to say that, but for Augustus, one would be lucky to be sure of one's father. But what is extraordinary—and yet typically Horatian—about these stanzas is the contrived regular alternation of perfectly plain statement in the odd verses with divine personification of abstractions—headed by one real goddess—in the even verses.[1] At any rate artistic μεταβολή is achieved here: but perhaps one might risk the reproach of fanciful speculation by claiming to see also a functional application of the pattern, as if Horace is equating the desirable world of fairy-tale (where Giant Wickedness always falls before heroic Good-Behaviour) with the contemporary scene where at last there is a place for honest toil and trade and blameless family life. Perhaps we are being induced to reflect that Augustus is building Utopia in Rome, or setting Roman life in Utopia.

Yet this scheme is itself only part of the imagery-pattern (the purely 'privative' pattern of presence versus absence) of the whole poem: it is maintained in the next stanza (25 ff.), where only *Germania* and *Hiberiae* are personified. On the other hand these three stanzas are countered by the last three,

---

[1] Hence my capitals. For *v.* 24 cf. ii. 16. 22, iii. 1. 39, and especially iii. 2. 31 f. *Faustitas* may therefore be defended against the strictures of Campbell, edn.[2] (1953), 141.

where, in each case, a mere suggestion of the figurative lurks—
the 'animating' of the vine and widower elms (30), the appeal
to myth (35 f.) and to poetic geography (40)—as a pinch of
salt in the plain fare all about. Prefacing this major antithesis
are four stanzas: the first has a plain, if allusive,[1] plea to the
Leader; the second a fulsome conceit and trope; then come
eight verses dedicated to an extended and delicate simile.
In all, a most complex formula.[2]

There are aspects of the use of imagery which are common
to all ancient poets, a fact which in itself precludes our seeking
the poet's self in his figures. For one thing, despite Aristotle's
πολὺ δὲ μέγιστον τὸ μεταφορικὸν εἶναι ... εὐφυΐας τε σημεῖόν ἐστι·
τὸ γὰρ εὖ μεταφέρειν τὸ τὸ ὅμοιον θεωρεῖν ἐστιν,[3] the classical
poet's impulse to note and dwell on a likeness previously unsuspected was a comparatively weak one. Homeric similes
(and there are virtually no Homeric metaphors) are contrived
pieces of engineering designed at once to punctuate and
decorate the oral narrative—and this is a large part of the
function of tragic stasima too, in their relation to the scenic
action—and, rather like the colourful gardens of country rail-
way stations, their considerable elaboration is a concern of
their own. Even when, after Homer, we pass to a more inte-
grated imagery with metaphor more in evidence, striking
freshness or audacity of stated or hinted relationships is rare.
It is sometimes said, and it may be true, that for the ancients
the place of honour—and, more, the functional importance—
we assign nowadays to imagery belonged rather to rhetoric,
to artificially enhanced *expression*; and further—and this may
well be in the main the cause of rhetoric's dominance—that
the classical poet's material was already highly poetical, the
objects of his natural world already to a considerable degree
'associated' and 'animated', so that the pathetic fallacy is no

---

[1] 'Divis' and 'Romulae' are *not* mythical here, of course. For 'sancto', see
Fraenkel, 442 n. 1.
[2] Roughly, and ignoring the kind of trope involved, the plan of plain and
figurative is, by stanzas: $p^f|f|f|f|pfpf|pfpf|pfpf|p^f|p^f|p^f$. (For the *thought*-plan, see
pp. 78 ff.: for the *style*-structure, see Fraenkel, 443.)   [3] *Poetics* 1459a5 ff.

arriviste or romantic notion in his work: rather, it would have
been a fallacy in him to ignore the animism and pretend that a
tree is a tree is a tree. Indeed Virgil's engrafted tree, surprised
to gaze on her new dress of alien leaves *et non sua poma*, or
the happy crops, or the politically minded bees, are commonplace: they need only to be credited with actual speech to
cross the frontier of fantasy and join the Aesopian geese and
foxes or the satiric Town and Country Mice—for these were
much less a fantasy to peoples accustomed to a numinous view
of nature and always too near to the animal world to separate
its life from their own.[1] And their world was more static: even
of the innovations, one could tell the ephemeral from the
lasting. For us even our σχήματα ἐκ τοῦ ἀδυνάτου are no longer
safe—it would be scarcely advisable to vow devotion to one's
poetic love till 'the sea shall yield corn' or 'the sun rise twice'
or 'men reach the moon', for land reclamation and supersonic
aircraft and the rocket engine have removed, or are tampering with, these impossibilities. Thus, because the imaginative
aspect of things was so much less separable from the things
themselves, it was that much harder for an ancient poet to use
imagery as handling-device or as a vehicle for a new way of
thinking about (or poetically experiencing) objective phenomena—although a new twist or a new combination of metaphors might vivify his work. By and large, he could just as well
experiment with purely linguistic rearrangements in his poetic
attempt to explore afresh the relationships of things. Hence the
extraordinarily nice classification and subdivision and regula-
tion of the figures and tropes of rhetoric[2] and the increasing
intoxication of Silver Latin authors with them. Furthermore,
'symbolisme' in its accepted sense—not but what the contributions to Huret's *Enquête* suggest that in its hey-day this term

[1] There are, of course, two related but opposed impulses: to assign human
reaction or rationality to animals, or even to plants or inanimate objects, as
often in the *Georgics* or Mr. Walt Disney's films; and to equate human behaviour, especially the less inhibited, with that of animals (as Medea δέργμα
λεαίνης ἀποταυροῦται, etc.).

[2] See, for convenience, the introduction to R. J. Getty's edn. of Lucan i,
lii ff.

meant all things to all men—was denied the Greeks and Romans. They could not use figurative speech as 'essentiellement un prodrome d'intuitivisme' (Mauclair), nor could they do as Baudelaire or Mallarmé, who attempt in their idiolect 'to convey a supernatural experience in the language of visible things, and therefore almost every word is a symbol and is not used for its common purpose but for the associations which it evokes of a reality beyond the senses'.[1] The metaphors of the ancients were too much part of the popularly accepted reality; they were commonly involved with myth and religion, as one sees from the depth of reference in, for instance, Horace's *debacchentur ignes*, where metaphor rests on religious observance, itself a web of imagery and figurative dogma. Their images, in fact, could scarcely be 'metaphors detached from their subjects', as Edmund Wilson has defined the symbolists' symbols. Besides, the Romans in particular had a characteristic national penchant for symbolic and summarizing and esoteric acts and rituals: hence all the 'business' with fetials' spears, praetors' rods, and witnesses' ears. That in their poetry abstract personifications should so behave themselves—Doom making play with adamantine nails, Death (or Proserpine) clipping a lock from a dying head—cannot be attributed, as a brilliant symbolic touch, to the revelation of any individual poet. Therefore, although their imagery is often personal, it is never private; although it is not superficial, it is not the raw stuff of thought either; and although it is diverse, it is readily classifiable and regulable. Hence the range of imagery of, say, a whole play may be critically handled under half-a-dozen rubrics.[2]

But the degree of control may vary, for the approximation

[1] C. M. Bowra, *The Heritage of Symbolism*, 5. See also A. G. Lehmann, *The Symbolist Aesthetic in France*; G. Michaud, *Message poétique du symbolisme*, ii, chap. vi.

[2] So Robert F. Goheen, *The Imagery of Sophocles' Antigone*, who also admits some functionalism of imagery (12 and 117), as differentiating characters by their idiosyncratic use of similar images. Medical imagery is especially widespread and striking in tragedy, the more so the less intimate the poet's connexion with the science: cf. Euripides' use of $\mu\nu\sigma\acute{\alpha}\tau\tau\omega\mu\alpha\iota$, or the collocation of $\kappa\alpha\rho\delta\acute{\iota}\alpha$ and $\ddot{\alpha}\sigma\eta$ (*Med.* 1149—see Page *ad loc.*—and 245, with which cf. Hippocrates *Epid.* 7. 10).

of poetic style, at least of the more dramatic, to unselfconscious speech makes such control more difficult; and it is not impossible to find whole sequences of centrifugal images, 'the images that come out of the central seed' (Dylan Thomas)— or perhaps better, 'tangential' images, the next in order each time breaking away from its predecessor to pursue briefly and fierily a course of its own. So in Io's distraught cry at Aeschylus, *Prometheus* 882 ff. the image of the racing car (τροχοδινεῖται δ' ὄμμαθ' . . . ἔξω δὲ δρόμου φέρομαι) gives way to a hint of a storm-tossed vessel (πνεύματι), whence her 'turbid words' (θολεροὶ λόγοι) themselves battle against the waves of madness (πρὸς κύμασιν ἄτης); so, in the prophecy of Darius' ghost, 'even the foundation of evils is not yet laid (κοὐδέπω κακῶν κρηπὶς ὕπεστιν) but those evils gush forth still like springs (ἀλλ' ἔτ' ἐκπιδύεται)—for so vast a congealed pool (πέλανος) of blood . . . etc.' (*Persae* 814 ff., rejecting Housman's emendation). Of this the converse is centripetal imagery, where the figures return to the centre for their inspiration and (from the critic's point of view) their explanation—and here enters the 'nuclear theory' which Norwood applies to Pindar, seeing the eleventh Pythian revolve entirely around the theme image of the Bee, or the Second Isthmian turn constantly inwards to the Silver Coin. This is sometimes treated as 'dominant' imagery, where one compelling revelation in the poet's mind pulls his comparisons and metaphors and ambiguities into conformity. For this recurrence one looks to the flowers in Sappho's work, or, more compactly, to the wild-beast motif which, so frequent in the *Bacchae*, passes at last to a psychopathic delusion in Agave.[1] But such 'dominance' is rare except in particular works or particular passages: so common and endemic are nine out of ten images that recurrence over a classical poet's entire corpus merely reflects recurrence over the whole of Greek or Latin literature.

---

[1] Sappho *frr.* 2, 94, 95, 96, 98, 105 L–P. See Dodds *ad* Eur. *Bacch.* 987–90. On sustained imagery in the *Oresteia*, and for a caution against overstressing it in interpretation, see D. W. Lucas, *The Greek Tragic Poets*,[1] 93 (and see the somewhat different presentation in the second edition, 118).

Where does Horace fit into this picture? He leaves us in no doubt about his capacity for vigorous and picturesque speech in the Satires and Epodes, but the linguistic level of the Odes is higher, and when coarser elements are excluded out goes much virility of simile or metaphor, too. And the linguistic *temperature* of the Odes is equally high, artificially so: after all, one can hardly, in all politeness, say less to a Glycera or a Lyde than *me lentus torret amor* or the like. The first feature that obtrudes itself is again the curious parallel existence of bold and tame, old and new:[1] love is a fire, to mate is to submit to Venus' yoke or to a fever, death is a sleep, the deer or hind illustrates all shrinking flight, youth is a fresh green shoot or an unripe grape, and so on, predictably and tediously. Yet there stand out, deriving their brilliance not merely from the foil of plain statement but equally from the wearisome un-originality of the common run of figures, gems of apt, bold, contemporary, and fresh imagination—the lictors are power-less to clear the mind's tumults from the path; an upright man's mind is a permanent consul; Regulus moves as un-concernedly to his doom as a *patronus* leaves for a well-earned vacation.[2] This feeling for composite texture at times produces extraordinary unevenness: in iii. 2. 17 ff. Virtue has figured in the typically Horatian guise of a successful Roman Warrior, owing nothing of his honoured position to the vagaries of electors—and then this same abstraction is somewhere in the skies, opening the gates of heaven for heroes (in Simonidean fashion),[3] itself exploring that forbidden path, and using wings to speed its journey. This effect is characteristic of Book IV: for

[1] For an inventory, see F. Schneider, 'Gleichnisse und Bilder bei Horaz', diss. Erlangen, 1914; A. Kiewadt, 'Vergleiche und Bilder in den Oden und Epoden des Horaz', diss. Greifswald, 1943. Also E. G. Wilkins, *CW*, 1935/6, 124 ff.

[2] ii. 16. 9 ff. (but hereabouts cf. Lucret. ii. 48 ff.); iv. 9. 34, 39 (helped, of course, by the popular etymology *qui recte consulat, consul cluat* Accius *apud* Varro, *LL* v. 80); iii. 5. 50 ff.

[3] This notion (of which iv. 8. 28 gives another version) is probably taken immediately from Simonides *fr.* 99 Bgk, 121 D. One may notice the Simonidean aphorism which begins the next stanza (*fr.* 66 Bgk, 38 D); and another lurks in *v.* 14 (*fr.* 65 Bgk, 12 D). On these, see Wilkinson, 113 n. 3, and W. J. Oates, 'The Influence of Simonides of Ceos upon Horace', diss. Princeton, 1932, chap. i.

here, even more markedly than in the earlier books, neologisms (*cinctutis non exaudita Cethegis*) like 'beluosus' or 'inimicat' jostle with archaisms (*priscis memorata Catonibus atque Cethegis*) such as 'adorea', 'spargier', 'quandoque'; or the occasional magniloquence ('tauriformis') balances the prosaic ('etenim').[1] In iv. 5 the imaginative elements are crude, derivative, and typical of authoritarian rule until we reach the humane, evocative simile of the mother watching and watching the shore for sight of her son's hoped-for return,[2] which makes up for all. In iv. 4 the progress of Hannibal is placed breathtakingly before us in the comparison of a pine-forest fire or the East Wind galloping over the waves; and *superbos* (*v.* 70) shows the arrogance of victory which so nearly was his and so nearly transmitted itself to his dispatches and their bearers: but these are gleams of something better in the midst of a depressing procession of animals—a positive zoo of imagery-creatures—eagle, sheep, snakes, roe, lion cub, bullocks, horses, eagles again, dove, stags, wolves, hydra, fire-breathing bulls.

We shall see later that one or two expressions are significantly repeated by Horace, as unmistakably summarizing an idea or evoking an atmosphere.[3] But they are few, and no image dominates him nor does any syndrome of images fall back on a central symbol in any ode:[4] to be sure i. 5 (*Quis multa gracilis te puer in rosa*) maintains at length the equation of a fickle mistress with a treacherous sea, and in ii. 5 (*Nondum subacta ferre iugum valet*) a young girl becomes poetically a heifer for most of the ode. But there is all the difference possible between this

---

[1] For -*ier* forms, see R. G. Austin *ad* Virg. *Aen.* iv. 493; for *quandoque*, Priscian iii, p. 138, 15 Keil; for *tauriformis*, Wilkinson, 132; for *etenim*, B. Axelson, *Unpoetische Wörter*, 123 n. 15.

[2] One may none the less speculate on the prehistory of this simile: for if the South wind is keeping the boy from home across the Carpathian Sea, where is the mother? Presumably in Egypt.

[3] See pp. 33 f. But it cannot be claimed that snow always evokes consideration of human old age, or tempests the storms of life: cf. to the contrary i. 2, ii. 16, iii. 17, iii. 25. Wine is a regular motif (see A. P. McKinley, 'The Wine Element in Horace', *CJ*, 1947, 229 ff.) but of differing application: cf. i. 7 with ii. 14.

[4] For an attempt so to analyse ii. 14, see Dahl, *CP* 1953, 240.

extension (of the theme-and-variation type) of a simple meta-phorical equation (carefully punctuated by neutral passages, or other images, as 'breathers' cf. i. 5. 10, ii. 5. 9–12) and the repeated affecting and levelling of heterogeneous parts of one's poetic discourse by the influence of some fixed inner symbol which forces all thought into its own terms. From this it must follow that Horace will find it no easier than any other ancient poet to use imagery as the basic means of handling ideas, al-though it may help him to universalize them. That is why it is hard to accept any fixed relation of even the mere presence of imagery to kinds of thought.[1]

As to centrifugal, or proliferating, imagery, Horace is again somewhat of a disappointment. True, he will pile up the figures (as in iv. 4, above) ; true, also, he will vary them in kind (as in i. 33 (*Albi ne doleas*) ἀδύνατον, myth, metaphor, and com-parison—each of respectable parentage—pass in turn before the reader in *vv.* 7–16). There is no question of ebullient thought either spurting out in startling figures, each fresh from the centre, or sparking off a series of images by chain reaction. Where Horace approximates to this, the result looks more like control that has suddenly failed, or an analogy pur-sued in greater detail than it can bear while remaining a con-sistent whole, or sometimes a simple confusion of two equally possible but incompatible visualizations.[2] In a fight for spoil

---

[1] Cf. M. Andrewes, *Greece and Rome*, 1950, 106 ff. She is correct in seeing that variation (i.e. of imagery) is never negligible ; but less easy to follow is her view that the presence of imagery is a matter of tact (at least the converse is untrue, as is shown by i. 6 and by the Gilbertian treatment, sardonic and highly figured, of the elderly *meretrices* Lydia and Lyce (i. 25, iv. 13), or of Chloris (iii. 15), who is still 'heavenly' in the sense of being a cloud!). Nor does the absence of imagery mean a lack of real feeling (there is practically no imagery in iii. 6. 20–44, but a genuine disgust is clear enough ; there is only enough hinted at to give poetic ὕψος to the words at iv. 11. 13–20, yet Horace's heart is given to Maecenas).

[2] Simple ambivalence is trivial : a tree may stand or fall, and be a symbol in either respect. The transitoriness of nature points one moral at ii. 9. 1–8 and ii. 10. 15–18, another at ii. 11. 9–12. At ii. 13. 13 f. the revealing *satis* suggests that with proper care men *might* dodge death (but contrast, *inter alia*, ii. 14 and iii. 1 and iv. 7) ; likewise the honest *raro* of iii. 2. 31 admits that sometimes crime does pay (as against iv. 5. 24).

between lioness and hunter in iii. 20 (*Non vides quanto moveas periclo*) which is pursued for ten verses, as one sees from *haec dentis acuit timendos*, it is startling, and even intriguing, to find the booty, which was a cub, becoming a human arbiter, beautiful, self-conscious and arrogant. In the sixth epode Horace will chase his vexers as a hound (*vv.* 5 ff.)—but soon grows horns (*v.* 12); while the hymn to Fortune (i. 35) not only shifts its representation of her from an impartial goddess to the personified 'Luck of the House' but invites us first to allow Fides (Loyalty) to see fit to leave that house, in hostile Fortune's company, then to censure the *vulgus infidum* for doing precisely the same.[1] Admittedly one notable success in this sphere appears at iv. 4. 61–68: the Roman race is seen by its foiled tormentor as a monster of the myths; yet, as he tries to drown it, it is beautified by the very water and becomes, almost imperceptibly, an athlete in the bloom of youth and health, wrestling his way to victory—and then, just as smoothly, a warrior whose exploits even the women at home will celebrate: but we have only to reflect that this has cleverly brought us back to the war-scene in which Hannibal began his speech to realize how artificial and unspontaneous the imagery is: here the use, the control, has triumphed. But for the most part Horace does less well. Necessitas indeed, rather like Virtus, is regularly unfortunate: as A. Y. Campbell sadly puts it (commenting on i. 35. 17 ff. in hope of emendation, to be sure) 'if Fate has been . . . equipped with the instruments here named' (timber-nails, wedges, clamp and molten lead) 'we do not need to have her provided with "a brazen hand" in order that she may operate them. On the contrary, any such artificial limb must be a severe handicap.'[2] Such incongruity is only too easy for any writer for whom imagery is mostly adventitious: for example, he may confuse a notion of sailing down the 'river

---

[1] But Fortuna will be the family prosperity, forced to leave, if *manicata* is read in *v.* 24, as Campbell conjectured. (Gow saw the weakness of *inimica* and aptly quotes *Epi.* ii. 1. 191 *trahitur manibus regum Fortuna retortis*: for the picture cf. Eur. *Hec.* 933 ff.)

[2] Edn.² (1953), 187 (iii. 24. 5 ff. have never been clear).

of time' towards the future with such a conception as 'time like an ever-rolling stream bears all its sons away', and forget that in the latter case, to us who watch from the bank, the river's mouth and all that is downstream is the *past*, and the upstream section, the water we have not seen, the *future*. Horace goes wrong on this (iii. 29. 33 ff.) and the word which gives him away is *retro* (*v.* 46)—for *fugiens hora vexit* shows he is continuing the simile in this stanza.[1]

To revert to the sea-imagery of Pyrrha's Ode (i. 5) or the heifer-motif of Lalage's (ii. 5), Horace ought not to go short of applause for having exploited his own simultaneous progress in two worlds of discourse: there is double-sense, practically punning in fact, in *aurae fallacis*,[2] *intemptata nites*, and *proterva fronte petit maritum*. Yet one should resist the temptation even to value this as we do Shakespeare's cleverness about the 'nag of Egypt' who,

> the breeze upon her, like a cow in June,
> hoists sails, and flies.[3]

Here there may be sketched a natural shift of thought, but the ambiguity is either a supervening effect in Horace or a calculated means towards apparent audacity of metaphor. It is not a prime cause of double-thinking; it is a play on words by one who rules them rather than a ruling of the poet's mind

---

[1] So Lucan at vii. 1–3 not merely introduces contemporary astronomy into his imagery, but simultaneously retains the normal poetic picture of the sun's chariot, driving from east to west. As the sun's own motion was scientifically regarded as being from west to east (as opposed to the east–west rotation of the heavens as a whole), there is the bizarre implication that the chariot is therefore always being dragged backwards through the sky despite the horses' efforts. (Critics who reject the interpretation of these verses as including the astronomical theory of the sun's counter-movement fall foul of *numquam magis*; those on the other hand who refuse to recognize the normal image here must trip over *retorsit*—cf. Ovid, *AA* i. 329 f.) This is compound confusion; but it well illustrates the hazards of the slightest attempts to develop 'consecrated images'.

[2] Cf. ii. 8. 21 f.

[3] *Antony and Cleopatra*, III. x. 14 f. Relevant is Day Lewis's pronouncement that 'the dramatic impulse will leap wider gaps between images than will the lyric or contemplative' (*The Poetic Image*, 83; and, for the inclusion of mixed metaphors, 47).

by his words. Horace, in fact, never—or very rarely, as in
Hannibal's speech in the Drusus-ode—Horace never forces the
reader, as bold metaphorists do, to accept his own interpretation (where it seems a novelty) of the natural continuity of
things. To do this is to battle with the reader and win: Horace
loses, or rather does not try to win. Hence a plurality of
images in the Odes normally gets, and deserves, the reproach
of incongruity.[1] His images stand *recto talo* when they are
single and traditional, or when they are reinforced by verbal
dexterity and point, or by contrastive organization (for sometimes he combines images, sometimes interjects an alien image,
sometimes again maintains a single figure throughout a piece
—these essays are to be seen, respectively at ii. 10, i. 5, ii. 20).
Of the three main sources of imagery—natural insight, 'consecrated images', and verbal shifts—Horace depends most by
far upon the third, and more on the second than the first.[2]

---

[1] Day Lewis (op. cit. 72 ff.) has some perceptive remarks on incongruity in
English poets, and states his own 'theory that image-patterns must in fact *be*
patterns and not random assemblages of word pictures' (74).

[2] Horace's use of myth runs in parallel fashion to his use of imagery generally.
He sometimes places himself very close to the mythical world; one thinks of
i. 17, iii. 7, iii. 4. But this does not astonish us who know Virgil's tenth eclogue
(or *vv.* 64 ff. of the sixth); and it is a common enough phenomenon in the
elegists. Perhaps it was a novel feature in the elegies of that self-dramatizing
personality, Gallus. (Unless Catullus lxviii. 91 ff. are relevant—there the poet's
own concerns are inset (*vv.* 91–100) in the myth of Laudamia which itself
enlivens and illustrates his love-story.) Myth, history, and contemporary life
make a triptych pattern in i. 12 (one readily conjures up *Aeneid* vi), and iv. 9 is
divided between the semi-mythical heroes and a flesh-and-blood contemporary
(as subjects for poetic canonization). And occasionally, as in i. 16 or ii. 4, some
tremendous myth exemplifies a human crisis which is really very small beer
indeed; the irony is typical.

That Horace, like Virgil, innovates—or seems to us to do so—is not unexpected, in view of the practice of, for instance, the Greek tragedians. He alone
keeps Prometheus in hell (ii. 13 and 18; cf. *Epo.* xvii), alone offers the *particulam
undique desectam* story (i. 16. 13–16), alone alludes to Thyestes' bitter death: at
Epo. xvi. 64 f. he ignores the silver age. As to the myth of Procne, the Greek
equations were: Procne = mother of Itys = nightingale and Philomela =
ravished sister = swallow (probably also in Plaut. *Rud.* 604). These received
a Virgilian twist into: Philomela = mother of Itys (*Ecl.* vi. 78), but Procne =
swallow (*G* iv. 15); yet Procne is still the mother of Itys for Ovid, *Met.* vi. 433,
etc. Horace equates the mother of Itys with the swallow (iv. 12. 5 ff.), and again
stands alone. We should not therefore be troubled by our inability to explain
some allusions, although editors have been swayed by this sort of consideration

But to show that much is mechanistic in his imagery, and that for it to be effective he needs a highly rational control, is not enough. Nor is it fair simply to hint at a programme of 'verbal shifts'. One will help criticism more by studying precisely how the sensitivity of expression which some poets achieved through an intuitive perception of unsuspected likeness is matched in Horace's lyric by experiments in the contrastive and combinatory potentialities of words. This attitude to composition will then be more readily recognized at all the levels at which the odes can be structurally analysed. Indeed, it may be worth making a case for Horace as a theorist on the subject of his own technique of word-employment, rather than merely an apt practitioner of the skills which *experientia* teaches. Of course, we may have to allow him the outlines of a theory and not a detailed scheme of linguistic analysis.

Nietzsche's pronouncement has had continual recrudescence in *Wortfügung* studies, which if acute and illuminating are yet oddly incomplete in some important respects. Corroboration of the niceness of Horatian word-placing stares the reader in the face from every page of the Odes. It may inspire a translator's emulation, like Milton's 'credulous, all gold'. The simplicity of *ut Proetum mulier perfida credulum falsis impulerit criminibus* is varied by the entwining, so wrath-provoking to a patriot, of *arva Marte coli populata nostro*, or by the emphatic horror of *utinam inter errem nuda leones!* But there are two quite

into tampering with the text at ii. 19. 24. It is the inconsistencies which are irksome, and Horace does not always conform to his own later rule *aut famam sequere aut sibi convenientia finge* (*AP* 119). Sometimes there exists a version of a myth which will nullify the whole point of an allusion (so twice at the close of iv. 7, in connexion with Hippolytus and Theseus—the latter suffering from the same discrepancy at Virg. *Aen.* vi. 122 and 617 f.). Most alarming is the virtually unbelievable role of Tithonus as a mortal at i. 28. 7 f., despite ii. 16. 30 where one trusts that *minuit* is a present tense! For to reverse without warning a stock *exemplum* is more shocking than simply to deny accepted facts. Incongruity and some maladroitness are again conspicuous, in fact. But Horace's welding of Greek and Roman mythology is not unusual; and even *Graia Camena* and *Calabrae Pierides* are nothing like so indigestible as Dante's 'o sommo Giove, che fosti in terra per noi crocifisso' (*Purg.* vi. 118 f.).

different kinds of verbal conjunction, of which these passages may serve as examples:

> qui *fragilem truci*
> commisit *pelago ratem*
>
> (i. 3. 10 f.)

and

> scatentem
> beluis pontum mediasque fraudes
> *palluit audax*
>
> (iii. 27. 26 f.).

Clearly, in the first quotation the effect is of heightened contrast and sharper meaning; but in the second there is, it appears, sheer paradox. Now parallel to this distinction of practical usage runs a theoretical dichotomy in Horace's own comment on the exploitation of words, that is, in his much discussed phrase *tantum series iuncturaque pollet* (*AP* 242).[1] Each of these terms, *series* and *iunctura*, denotes an activity whose result is to revivify known and common words, reminting the worn coin: *ex noto fictum carmen sequar . . . tantum de medio sumptis accedit honoris*. It is clear, too, that while *iunctura* is included in the general notion of word-ordering (*in verbis etiam tenuis cautusque serendis* / *dixeris egregie notum si callida verbum* / *reddiderit iunctura novum AP* 46 ff.),[2] it is set apart as a distinct and dominant process.

Perhaps it will not be too bold to adduce at this point a

---

[1] The reference in the last footnote may suggest that the *Ars Poetica* is not evidence for Horace's poetic practice (on this epistle in general, see Wilkinson, 95 ff.; on its own structure, Tracy, *Greece and Rome*, 1948, 104 ff.). But it is easy to draw a line between its precepts for scenic poetry and its general theorizing on *Dichtersprache*, and on the latter we are free to speculate as to Horace's consistency. What needs to be rejected is such flat-footed criticism as would refuse to see these odes as 'articulated' and divisible into parts for interpretative purposes through too literal attachment to *denique sit quodvis, simplex dumtaxat et unum* (23).

[2] Very acceptable would be Bentley's transposition of *vv.* 45 and 46, effectively separating *iunctura* from *verba serere*. Still, despite his acidity about the nearness of *verbis . . . verbum* in the mss. tradition, *v.* 45 as it stands (*hoc amet, hoc spernat*, etc.) refers to the *choice* of words, which is not the sense of *serere*. It is safer to leave the text alone, noting that *etiam* shifts the topic from thematic to verbal ordering. (That *series* means contiguous succession is clear from *innumerabilis annorum series*, iii. 30. 4 f.).

manner of thinking common to most modern general linguists:
for, although adherents of different schools diverge drastically,
even pugnaciously, over the methods and even the aims of
analysis, there are certain principles which are widely accepted
and curiously revealing to the Horatian student. The so-called
'glossematic' group (of Copenhagen) stress above all that contrastive substitution is the key to the establishing of the operational categories of a language. This principle is applied to
language-analysis at its three levels—of sounds, of grammar,
and of lexicon. It is crucial, for instance, that 'pin' differs from
'tin', for from this one finds, and by this one justifies the finding, that *p* and *t* are distinctive speech-sounds in English
(although the speech-sounds are distinctive in groups, and it is
more properly said that this particular *p* and *t* belong to different groups). Again, at the grammatical level, the difference
between 'helps' and 'helped' is of function as well as of form,
and this motivates the setting up of '*-s*' and '*-ed*' as opposed
elements in the operation of the English verbal system. Thus,
among the lexical items, the important fact about 'moon' is
that it is capable of being contrastively substituted in this way
for 'tree' or 'stone' or other items. To be sure, this school
thinks very largely in terms of the inventories of items which
may 'commute' like this (that is, produce, by replacing one
another, changes of content as of expression) at various positions in the utterance, and consequently deals not only with
utterances analysed as to the relation of their parts but also with
'columns', as it were, of commuting items. That is to say, one
lists *p*, *t*, *k*, etc. as possibilities at the position '( )in', or, to
return to whole words, the items 'man', 'boy', 'fellow', 'worker',
etc. (but not 'cheese' or 'chimney') at the position 'Jack is a
fine ( )'. But the essential factor is the importance of the
whole utterance—the sentence, in practice—whether for the
analysis of the items within it in their relation to one another
(the horizontal axis, so to speak)—as is obvious enough—or for
the listing and classifying of the commuting items at various
positions (the vertical axis): the lists come from, and must be

re-applied to, the total utterance. In fact, the commuting items have been extracted by the analyst from his comparison of otherwise apparently identical utterances; these are not necessarily spontaneous utterances which occur in his hearing, for time is too short to attain this ideal except rarely, but if they are invented they are tested by the readiness of a native speaker to accept or reject them as possibilities for his language.

Now the horizontal and vertical axes are common to the methodologies of all schools. But it is not surprising to find greater weight assigned to the horizontal, as for example in most American treatments. These are sufficiently homogeneous to be called, as a whole, 'distribution-conscious'. For, as 'commutation' is the meaningful interplay of linguistic items within the vertical lists—the relation, in fact, of 'fence' to 'tree' or to 'nest' in the sentence 'the bird sits on the (   )'—so 'distribution' refers to the occurrences of the items within the utterances under review, and to the comparison of the range of contexts possible for each item—that is, in our example, to the co-occurrence of 'bird' and 'sits' and 'nest', and to the differing context-ranges of 'bird' on the one hand and, say, 'horse' or 'bicycle' on the other. The position within an utterance at which an item occurs is therefore a matter of basic study in both Danish and American analysis, and the schools really differ only in the degree of importance which they attach to this horizontal dimension as such.[1]

The most influential English school of recent years characterizes the two-axis relationship by the terms 'structure' and 'system', but again places greater stress on the structural or horizontal axis. In describing the nature and operation (which

---

[1] The Americans prefer to establish operational elements, not by separating commuting items but by gathering together items which are not found in identical environments (hence the term 'complementary distribution'), such as the *t*-sounds of *tea, too, try*, etc. This works well enough for sounds and forms; less well for lexis, for most words contrast singly rather than in groups of contextual variants, and quite often what is formally one word is found in contrastive environments (polysemy), or formally distinct words occur in identical contexts with no contrast of meaning (synonymy). Consequently this type of theorizing is less often applied to word-meaning.

are the same thing) of an item, account is to be taken, above all, of the other items which are present along with it in the utterance, and the meaning of the item derives from that of the utterance. At the lexical level, therefore, the meaning of a word is often defined as 'its use in the language' or its 'privilege of occurrence' in contexts; and this latter may be very limited or very free, for meaning is largely quantitative—one may compare the potentialities of 'boy' and 'sand-boy', for the second demands the single context 'happy as a ( )'. One must, with this approach, apprehend the meaning of each word first by noting 'the company it keeps', and secondly by relating the whole utterances in which the word is embedded to the situational contexts in which the utterances are made. For mere 'object'-words ('table', 'cat', etc.) it is rather by the second criterion that one achieves an immediate result—a certain recognizable animate object will be found to be present in the situations where an utterance including the word 'cat' is made. But for other classes of words the first consideration is the vital one; and these appearances in the same linguistic context, these 'mutual expectancies' (at the lexical level, when the analyst is concerned with words as dictionary entries, so to put it) are termed 'collocations'.[1] Dictionaries, in practice,

---

[1] The reader may acquaint himself with these hypotheses in the following sources: L. Hjelmslev, *Omkring Sprogteoriens Grundlaeggelse* (=*Prolegomena to a Theory of Language*, translated by Francis J. Whitfield in Memoir 7, *Internat. Journal of American Linguistics* (1953)); B. Siertsema, *A Study of Glossematics*; B. Bloch and G. L. Trager, *Outline of Linguistic Analysis* (esp. 42–45); Zellig S. Harris, *Methods in Structural Linguistics* (esp. 5)—somewhat redressed by C. F. Hockett, *Course in Modern Linguistics*, who stresses contrast, esp. for sounds; L. Wittgenstein, *Philosophical Investigations* (trans. Anscombe), §§ 43, 80, 109 (but his is a qualified view: 'for a *large* class of cases—though not for all—in which we employ the word "meaning" it can be defined thus: the meaning of a word is its use in the language'); J. R. Firth, 'Modes of Meaning', now in *Papers in Linguistics 1934–1951*, 190 ff. (esp. 194 ff.). The term 'collocation', in this specialized application, is Firth's, as (among others quoted) is the useful 'mutual expectancy'; the grammatical equivalent 'colligation', to which word-boundaries are as such irrelevant, belongs to H. F. Simon, *Bulletin of the School of Oriental and African Studies*, 1953, 327 f.; see also Firth's remarks in *Studies in Linguistic Analysis*, 11 ff.

These ideas are, in general terms, fairly universal: thus in the recent Russian treatment of V. A. Zvegintsev, *Semasiologija*, Moscow, 1957, word-meaning is

when not being frankly historical and derivation-minded, tend merely to list optional *varianda*: their true task is to quote the acceptable collocations of the words under review, as exhaustively as can be afforded.

It has seemed worth while bringing in as evidence these theoretical concepts of contemporary language-analysis because they may make clear an important feature in Horace's own methods of poetic composition. *Series* has to do with nothing more than the actual order of words on the tongue or the page: its effects are dynamic, in the sense that they constitute variations of the power or weight or impact or sharpness of the words used. The insertion of the fragile craft into the hostile sea is visibly or audibly enhanced; the wolf is shown to us actually among the (divinely encouraged) lambs—*inter audaces lupus errat agnos*—and so on.[1] Making profit even of the necessity of adding an epithet to *aer* to restore it to its Homeric sense of 'mist', Horace sets himself in his fright and his saviour-deity's action actually within the 'smoke-screen' which was so opportunely produced on Philippi's field (ii. 7. 14 *denso paventem sustulit aere*).

But there stands apart the exploitation seen in *palluit audax* or *facili saevitia* or *rura . . . mordet aqua taciturnus amnis*. And here the actual contiguity of the words is basically unimportant as compared with the vividness, the excitement, and the novelty engendered by the simple fact that we do not expect these words to occur together at all, that in fact they stand in each case in an unfamiliar or paradoxical collocation—and this can hardly be anything but an exercise in *iunctura*.[2] Whether Horace states *iunctura* as being one aspect of the general process of *verba serere* or, as Bentley would have it, separates *series* and *iunctura* entirely, it is reasonable to understand in his theory

similarly defined purely in terms of the combinatory possibilities of one word with others (see esp. 123; the key-word is *sočetanija*).

[1] See Wickham's note on this kind of effect, on ii. 4. 1–12. i. 5. 1 is a famous example, too, as is *S* ii. 6. 80 f.

[2] The literal meaning of *iunctura* is 'joint' or 'joining', and this (as applied to sounds) seems to be Quintilian's employment of it at ix. 4. 33 ff.

two interrelated but distinct matters of method. And the latter can, as the former cannot, achieve the same sort of impact as do neologisms: to deal with emergencies, Horace declares (*AP* 48 ff.), a circumspect invention of words, itself soundly based on comparative philology and consisting of derivatives or calques, will be permitted. But he prefers to leave invention or resuscitation to *Usus* (*Epi.* ii. 2. 119; *AP* 70 ff.) : and ingenuity of collocation (*callida iunctura*), renovating the familiar (*notum si . . . verbum reddiderit . . . novum*), is for him the outstanding achievement (*dixeris egregie*).

The two processes, *series* and *iunctura*, being separate, can be employed together to increase the impact of the expression. Apart, they may each be enhanced by another contrived effect, as when in *immitis Glycerae* the effect of the collocation depends in turn on a learned *figura etymologica*, or as in *quae caret ora cruore nostro?* the *series* is assisted by the sounds. But together they have an immense force. That is, indeed, why *palluit* and *audax*, impinging so much more on mind and memory than *inaudax . . . raptor* (iii. 20. 3 f.), are set cheek by jowl, for here the *series*-feature (always a powerful asset in an inflected language) corroborates the major effect of *iunctura*. Conversely, in *inter audaces lupus errat agnos* the major contribution is that of *series*, but *iunctura* plays its subordinate role there too (*audaces agnos!*). Of course, all poets do these things: but Horace sees them as parts of a mechanical process, susceptible of theoretical analysis and statement, and says so.[1] His adroitness in their

---

[1] Wilkinson (126) remarks that 'those have been on the right track who have held that *iunctura* includes "metaphor-making" '. True; and they, and he, deserve credit. (He has deserved credit, too, since this chapter was first written, for his term 'semantic collocation'—an elaboration of Wickham's 'setting'—as an equivalent for *iunctura*, and for his inventory of occurrences, in *CQ*, 1959, 186 ff.). Most writers, however, have seen no more in the term than 'word-placing': so even the author of the only book known to me to be entirely dedicated to this problem, F. Cupaiuolo's *A proposito della 'callida iunctura' oraziana* (1942). It is heartening to see that the *Thesaurus ling. Lat.* commonly introduces the verbal collocations in which the word under review is found under the rubric 'iuncturae'.

It may be worth pointing out that the nouns, verbs, and adjectives, above all, in a language operate in relatively open commutation, but with a tendency to

application, his 'felicity', is therefore carefully controlled and —if one thinks but of (*hiems*) *oppositis debilitat pumicibus mare* (where *iunctura*, *series*, and choriambic rhythms each supply an essential part to the completed product) or *bacchante . . . vento* or *non ego te, candide Bassareu, invitum quatiam*—it is adventurous, too, although with limitations which will soon appear. And so we may draw the comforting conclusion that Petronius (*curiosa felicitas*) and Quintilian (*felicissime audax*) were both right.

But some critics contrive to be more right than others; and within the *quidlibet audendi potestas* claimed for poets by others Horace has his reservations of theory and practice, and Quintilian may have gone too far. Mechanistic application of the twin postulates of combination and contrast is the whole secret of Horace's composition; natural impulses to re-order phenomena, flashes of perceptive insight, these do not enter into it. The implications of this approach become clearer by consideration of an uncomfortable passage:

> non rura quae Liris quieta
> mordet aqua taciturnus amnis.
>
> (i. 31. 7 f.)

Those who reject this image on 'common-sense' grounds would do well to remember Lucretius' *ripas radentia flumina rodunt* (v. 256); but their suspicions are not ill-founded. What is wrong is the actual inclusion of *aqua* as the instrument of the metaphorical process: not even the acceptability of this *iunctura* as

closure; thus we reject all but 'field', 'land' and a few similar items from the context 'I plough the ( )'. Metaphor could be defined as the reopening of these lists of commuting terms; hence, 'plough the sea' or ' . . . sky' or whatever the user chooses—'vertical man', 'green thoughts', and the rest. After the restrictive influence of the situations of everyday life has thus once been defied, there will tend to be another limitation of the collocational possibilities, this time definable as the sum of the collocations so far combined (i.e. those of 'plough' plus those of 'sea', those of 'green' plus those of 'thought'). If, in this new-style utterance, there follows another extension of commuting terms at another position, and this before all sense of novelty has been lost from the earlier extension, then we have the 'mixed metaphor', which has earned surprisingly bitter reproaches since Quintilian (viii. 6. 50). These definitions say nothing of the acceptability of such locutions or of the nature of the poet's impulse so to speak and write; they are merely a metalinguistic device for handling the phenomena.

a whole can stand up to this combination of unfamiliarity and familiarity (not to say literalness). You cannot bite with water: and the ordinary man knows too much about biting and about water to be talked into supposing that you can. A metaphor springing from an intuitive equation of certain aspects of two different activities will exclude automatically any term which, by being too explicit, inevitably hinders the acceptance of the equation. Collocation-imagery may well be too pedestrian and too honest to make the suppression and succeed. What is more, we read elsewhere in the Odes not only *villaque flavus quam Tiberis* lavit (ii. 3. 18) but also *quae loca fabulosus* lambit *Hydaspes* (i. 22. 7 f.)—which indicates that, despite the logical implications of his theory, Horace builds fresh sets of collocations (and therefore extends the lists of commuting items) even though these nullify, by their own parallel existence, the novelty and power of each by itself. By these experiments[1] Horace makes his own poetic impact more diffuse; comparable is the trio of *mors et fugacem* persequitur *virum* (iii. 2. 14), *Culpam Poena* premit *comes* (iv. 5. 24), *ver* proterit *aestas* (iv. 7. 9, and cf. truditur *dies die* at ii. 18. 15 or urget *diem nox et dies noctem* at *Epo.* xvii. 25). Horace is working variations on a theme, a typical trait: he combines them in *comes atra* premit sequiturque *fugacem* (*S* ii. 7. 115). It is as if he were inviting commendation for the number of replacements he can conceive, but with an ear cocked for some applause for boldness.[2] This is entirely in accordance with his grammatical experiments, wherein the formula *noli quaerere* is diversified in such colligations as *mitte sectari, fuge quaerere, remittas quaerere,* and similarly *animus . . . oderit curare* and *quaerere distuli*: one may no doubt compare *penna metuente solvi*. It is in this way that the surprising *nescias an te generum beati Phyllidis flavae decorent parentes* (ii. 4. 14) is derived from the stereotyped first person *nescio an* construction.[3] Similarly *neglegens ne qua populus laboret* (iii. 8. 25)

[1] Which have something in common with Quintilian's *transumptio* (viii. 6. 37 ff.).
[2] After all, scholars may unearth prior authority for a metaphor more often than Horace was aware of it.   [3] Cf. Campbell, edn.[2] (1953), 47.

represents an extension of the *ne*-clause structure, regular with *cavere*, to its opposite *neglegere* (i.e. *non cavere*), rather as the type *fac cogites* etc. induces *cave existimes* etc. (instead of *cave ne . . .*).[1] Thus, to revert to metaphor, even the seemingly startling and superbly apt picture of the ageing Lyce as *dilapsam in cineres facem* depends on all the many occurrences of that hackneyed collocation-type exemplified by *urit me Glycerae nitor, arsit Atrides . . . virgine rapta,* and (more immediately) *me torret face mutua . . . Calais.* In another way, too, Horace makes his replacements gentle, by easing the *iunctura* with the help of explanatory elements set within it. Thus he writes *nutrit rura Ceres almaque Faustitas,* where *alma (alo)* 'glosses' *nutrit;* or *Thracio bacchante . . . vento,* where *Thracio* smooths the path for *bacchante.*

Another feature which is good evidence for Horace's one-foot-on-the-ground flights of poesy is that 'double-barrelled language' or *Doppelsinn* which has not gone unnoticed by commentators.[2] *Tumultus mentis* is a surprising collocation inasmuch as *tumultus* is common in contexts where the reference is to civil uproar and physical struggles: but it is made easier to receive by the adjacent *consularis summovet lictor* (ii. 16. 9 f.) which makes it at home in the context. *Rigidi Getae* will invite a normal interpretation of their epithet as 'living in a wintry climate': yet at the same time the total context (the entire ode, in fact, iii. 24) imposes the sense of 'censorious, inflexible', as with Ovid's *rigidus censor (AA* ii. 664). It is notable here, in point of method, that Horace combines two collocations, a familiar and a new, so that the one, so to speak, sponsors the other. This is why there appears so often the figure we call

---

[1] Rather than the scholiast's gloss *non timens* (for that semantic jump is greater). Note *parce cavere* in the next verse.

[2] Especially noted by Andrewes, *CR*, 1948, 111 ff. *Frigidas noctes . . . agit* (iii. 7. 6 ff.), as explained in this article, well exemplifies the process described above ('loveless', made easier to accept by the alternative sense 'really cold'). In *sublimi anhelitu* (i. 15. 31) double-sense is probable, but the technical medical meaning of 'shallow breath' (see *LSJ s.vv.* μετάρσιος, μετέωρος) springs less readily to mind than the imaginative (as Gow says, 'with panting head up-reared'). The twofold reference of *ignis* at *Epo.* xiv. 13 is intriguing. (See also Wilkinson, *CQ*, 1959, 188 f.)

'zeugma', where the lexical or grammatical connexions are accepted and regular for at least part of the utterance—thus *multa sodalibus*, nulli plura . . . dividit *oscula* etc. (i. 36. 5 f.).

It is no use pretending that Horace's recourse to imagery is, for the most part, anything but a permutation of words, and conducted moreover on principles almost painfully rational and systematic, sound though they may be. Perhaps the human spirit, with the Muses' help, should soar freely or swoop surprisingly; but there can be exhilaration in the short, careful, and two-dimensional moves on a chess-board. It is curious, therefore, that a programme which of itself could produce a breathtaking poetic idiolect is neutralized by a typically Roman 'safety first' policy in application. Yet this ambivalence accords well with all that was seen to be true of Horace's technique of word-usage, where the poetry results from Heraclitean tensions between bold and tame, new and old, intricate and simple. The single underlying law is that each element in his poetic discourse shall as far as possible derive its force from, and be set off by, another, and nothing work singly or exist for its own sake.

The supervening effects of all this can themselves be endlessly subdivided and catalogued. 'Catachresis', 'hyperbole', 'oxymoron', for example, are nothing more than different aspects of *iunctura*, as are 'hyperbaton' or 'anastrophe' of *series*. That is why Horace is noticeably *varius figuris* for anyone who is figure-minded. One of these figures (or tropes) deserves special attention, if only because it demonstrates *in nuce* how tightly Horace controls his locutions, and how he experiments with them. It shows, too, a way of varying collocations without really disturbing the accepted inventory of such for a given word: 'imagery without tears', in fact. And the trope which concerns us here is *hypallage*.

The general rubric of hypallage covered a diversity of phenomena. There is included metonymy of the types *pericula Martis* or *Africa quae . . . incultius agebat*;[1] or again 'mutua

---

[1] Cf. Cicero, *Orator* 27, 93. (The metonymy of Africa is at Sallust, *Jugurtha* 89.)

casuum permutatio' like *dare classibus Austros*. Indeed, a 'conceit' is sometimes firmly established, as when *qui pectore tela transmittant* or *vir, qui per ferrum . . . evasit* emerges from the common basic play of transferring motion from the moving to the stationary body.[1] This particular example finds an adjectival application in Virgil's *sagitta . . . volucris diverberat auras* (*Aen.* v. 502 f.) ; and hypallage κατ' ἐξοχήν resides in this deceptively simple device of transference of epithet. Horace increases but controls its use, and is neither as sparing as his predecessors nor as lavish and automatic as his Silver successors; he can still be subtle and modestly daring.

Simple hypallage of this kind needs no seeking but offers itself on every page—*iratos . . . regum apices, iracunda Iovem ponere fulmina, lividos distinguet Autumnus racemos . . . varius, heres . . . mero tinguet pavimentum superbo*, and many more (nor is the transference always from the living thing, as *Chimaerae spiritus igneae* shows). It is worth calling attention, though, to two points. First, that Horace is characteristically developing an exciting product from a cautious process. The process is in each case a rearrangement of the grammatical colligations which does not disturb the total lexical collocation(s), for the contextual combination *rex+apex+ira* is in no way unusual in itself, nor is *Iuppiter+fulmen+ira*, nor (*heres+superbus*)+(*merum +pavimentum*). The product, however, of the grammatical shifts is imagery of no little force and considerable summarizing value, for the diadems enshrine the imperiousness of kings as the thunderbolts carry the fire and might of Jupiter, while 'mottled Autumn' evokes successfully the human instinct for pictorial animism ('wrinkled Care', 'Laughter holding both his sides'). Secondly, within this perfectly common and normal transference there is room for that calculated ambiguity (ἀμφι-βολή, *ambiguitas*) which poets sometimes use.[2] Much puzzlement has been occasioned by the phrase about *superbos Tarquini*

---

[1] See the discussion and references in R. J. Getty's comment on Lucan i. 212.

[2] Cf. *CP*, 1955, 167. At iii. 6. 22 *fingitur artibus* may point simultaneously to social accomplishments, affectations and pretences, and make-up.

fasces, where interpretation by transference seems inescapable and, clashing with what history tells us of the introduction of the fasces, fuses Priscus and Superbus in enigmatic fashion.[1] Another aspect of this linguistic freedom is visible in sequences like *doctus sagittas tendere Sericas arcu paterno* (i. 29. 9 f.) where the epithets owe no special allegiance to their partner nouns, indicating simply that the captive boy's prosperous days lay in the (broken) reign of his father and in (now far-off) China. Comparable is *Achaico* at iv. 3. 5, or *Sabellis* at iii. 6. 38: each gives the setting. More clearly still, the villain whom *crediderim . . . penetralia sparsisse nocturno cruore hospitis* (ii. 13. 5 ff.) performed his fell deed in the depth of night—and the adjective which says so might be attached to any of the nouns in the phrase at all. Horace feels, it appears, that in a syntagm which has a verbal nucleus all the grammatical relationships are ultimately adverbial.[2]

On this ground-theme, simple epithet transfer, Horace works variations. A very understandable shift, and by no means peculiar to him, is that to double hypallage. Virgil indulges in it, describing the portals of Iarbas' shrines as *variis florentia limina sertis* (*Aen.* iv. 202) when in sober fact it is the doors which are gaily decorated and the flowers are in the fillets. Lucan's *Arctoo spumantem vertice Rhenum* (i. 371), as well as having exaggeration, exchanges its adjectives in just this way. The formula finds its equivalent expression in the Odes: so *amicus Aulon fertili Baccho* (ii. 6. 18 f.), although really it is the god's befriending which has given the hill its fertility; and perhaps too, when *imprimeretque muris hostile aratrum exercitus insolens* (i. 16. 20 f.), the army alone is hostile and the plough only so in their hands, being in itself a sign of arrogant and wilful destruction. The curious may unearth more of the same

---

[1] i. 12. 34 f. See Fraenkel, 295 n. 2 (and for the 'Virgilian' ambiguity, cf. 440 n. 2—a trait which might defend the two Africani of iv. 8. 16 f.). The adjective *superbus* is frequently in hypallage in the Odes (i. 37. 31, ii. 14. 27, iv. 4. 70, iv. 15. 7).

[2] For the common adverbial function of an adjective, see E. C. Woodcock, *A New Latin Syntax*, § 88 and note; and compare the types *vespertinus ursus*, τριταῖοι ἀφίκοντο, etc.

pattern, and will find again how Horace's adroitness enlivens his mechanics: the characterization of Damalis is forceful and witty enough, for she, while all bend yearning eyes upon her, *nec . . . novo divelletur adultero, lascivis hederis ambitiosior* (i. 36. 18 ff.). The *figura etymologica* ('ambit') is part of the joke, but as Damalis has won for herself the attribute which nature and literature give the ivy ('the female ivy so enrings the barky fingers of the elm'), by a stylistic but scarcely equitable exchange the unoffending plant is assigned the girl's wantonness.[1]

Another variation (suppressed hypallage) is brother to that metonymy of which *barbarus Araxes* is a typical instance, the river denoting its locality and the people who live there, and bearing for them the (adverse) epithet. There is still fairly strict control of the linguistic experiment; but if the full hypallage of *furvae regna Proserpinae* is regarded as the source-type, we may perhaps allow ourselves to see (by way of development) a frequent daring suppression of one noun in the 'eternal triangle'. Thus *vitrea Circe* is 'Circe, quae vitreum *mare* incolit', *Dianae celebris die* is 'illo die, quo Diana *templum* videt celebre,' and *vivae* (or *vigiles*) *lucernae* are not directly personified, but have accepted a shift of the revellers' wakefulness on to the lamps which aid their revels. From this line of attack upon imagery come such results as *albus Notus*, or *candidi Favonii, decorae palaestrae, pallida Mors, informis hiemes*, and *bruma*

---

[1] I cannot help recording a suspicion that the surprising phrase *princeps Aeolium carmen ad Italos deduxisse modos* (iii. 30. 13 f.) depends likewise on double hypallage. The 'carmen' was Latin; its national character is abundantly clear and not only for the Roman Odes, and a Greek beginning ('motto') always quickly fades into a Roman development (i. 18, i. 37, *et saep.*). The metres were Greek; Catullus' sapphics barely count, and Horace's own modifications of the Lesbian rhythms does not make them 'Itali modi'. i. 32. 3 ff. gives us what we expect: 'age, dic *Latinum*, barbite, *carmen*, *Lesbio* primum *modulate* civi'. That Horace could *later* claim to have become 'Romanae fidicen lyrae' (iv. 3. 23) and 'Latinus fidicen' (*Epi.* i. 19. 32 f.)—cf. Fraenkel, 409, and Ovid, *Tristia* iv. 10. 50 for 'Ausonia lyra'—justified his *envoi* to the first publication (and iv. 3. 12 and 23 quote iii. 30. 13 f.). But when he actually penned iii. 30 he may well have been 'underwriting' a piece of bravado by means of a stylistic figure, just as the bravado of the opening verses is 'underwritten' by the notably diffident 'run-down' in the rest of this usually misunderstood ode (see pp. 69 f.). At all events, we are not here presented with the mere vagueness of Propertius' claim *Itala per Graios orgia ferre choros* (iii. 1. 4).

iners,[1] with the sky, the athletes, the corpse, the fields, and the farmer, if unexpressed, at once leaping in reassuring fashion to the reader's mind. Interesting essays in trope, all of these: but under close control and to that extent the more tame as *iunctura*. Yet Horace again makes up for much by his wit: Tyndaris no doubt hopes that the closing words of her invitation to the Sabinum

nec metues protervum

suspecta Cyrum, ne male dispari
incontinentis iniciat manus
    et scindat haerentem coronam
crinibus *immeritamque vestem*

(i. 17. 24 ff.)

are cast by their author in this elliptical-transfer mode. But Horace leaves it open to each reader ungallantly to refuse the figure and to take the last two words literally—as if the girl's clothes, at least, have done nothing to deserve rough treatment.

Even so, not all Horace's lyric idiolect is so mathematical and permutable. Some expressions answer quite regularly to a particular atmosphere or a particular emotional reaction.[2] Consider these collocations:

iam pauca aratro iugera regiae
moles relinquent

(ii. 15. 1 f.)

immemor struis *domos*
*maris*que Bais obstrepentis urges
summovere litora

(ii. 18. 19 ff.)

[1] Cf. *uncta palaestra*, Ovid, *Her.* 19. 11. Gow (xxiv) points to the causative force thus assigned to the epithets, whether the source-noun is present or not, by the transfer of a proleptic adjective: of this, *inaequali tonsore (Epi.* i. 1. 94) is perhaps the classic example. The *nigri venti* of i. 5. 7 take their epithet from the (here included) sea whose brightness they dim—cf. Homer's φρὶξ μέλαινα. At ii. 8. 15 f. Cupid's arrows derive their description as *ardentis* partly from their effect on the victim (the 'ardeo aliqua' *iunctura*), partly by double but oddly literal hypallage: the whetstone is in fact the source of their heat, they in turn in fact stain it with blood.

[2] So one may usefully study *proles* in the Odes (cf. iii. 6. 38, iv. 5. 23, iv. 15. 27, *CS* 19 and 47; iv. 6. 1 stands apart, but its divine associations are consonant enough with the other occurrences).

> non humilis *domos*
> *fastidit* . . .
> contracta pisces *aequora* sentiunt
> iactis in *altum molibus*; huc frequens
> *caementa* demittit redemptor
> cum famulis dominusque terrae
> *fastidiosus* . . .
>
> cur invidendis postibus et novo
> sublime ritu *moliar* atrium?
>
> (iii. 1 *passim*)
>
> *caementis* licet occupes
> terrenum omne tuis et *mare* publicum
> (iii. 24. 3 f.)
>
> *fastidiosam* desere copiam et
> *molem* propinquam nubibus arduis
> (iii. 29. 9 f.)

where one picture, summarizing the materialistic, feverish, and ruthless malaise of the unphilosophic rich, presents itself throughout. By building such *iuncturae* Horace gives himself the power to use words taken from them in a highly personal significance, carrying their Horatian meaning into the fresh context over and above such sense as their collocations in the language at large has given them: and that is why

> vis consili expers mole ruit sua
> (iii. 4. 65)

conveys not merely the analogy of a collapsing house (*ruit*) but all the brashness and excess he castigates in those who are powerful in worldly matters alone (*mole*). And why are these same uneasy, unthinking men of wealth, in the course of a lecture on the humbler homes of a more virtuous and austere age, told that

> nec fortuitum spernere *caespitem*
> leges sinebant
> (ii. 15. 17 f.)

if not to drive home to them that something of the gods must enter into the making of a home? For *caespes* is, for Horace, a word at home in religious *iuncturae*: so

> hic vivum mihi caespitem, hic
> verbenas, pueri, ponite turaque
> bimi cum patera meri
>
> (i. 19. 13 ff.)

and

> flores et acerra turis
> plena . . . positusque carbo in
> caespite vivo
>
> (iii. 8. 2 ff.)

and this adds something essential to the 'house-building' context, beyond the mere 'thatch' sense of, say, *tuguri congestum caespite culmen* (Virg. *Ecl.* i. 68).[1]

Only these cases, and an occasional neologism, contradict the judgement that Horace's poetic language presents nothing out of the way, nothing, that is, that could not be solved even with the aid of a Latin dictionary, if such existed, compiled by one who had never read the Odes. The noteworthy features of this lyric creation, at this level, are the theoretic and mechanistic approach, the exploitation of contrast and combination, and the strict control. These considerations should inform our own criticism of these poems equally at other levels.

---

[1] That *caespes* quite often carries a religious aura is, of course, true; cf. *inter alia* Virg. *Aen.* iii. 304 f., Val. Flacc. v. 61, Sil. Ital. xvi. 43, Martial i. 88. 2, v. 34. 9, Tacitus, *Germ.* 27, *Ann.* i. 62, and Servius, *ad Aen.* xii. 119 ('Romani enim moris fuerat caespitem arae superimponere'). Horace is giving dominance in his own idiolect to a pattern of collocation which occurs, with less comparative frequency, outside it.

II

Contrast-technique 1: The Order of the Odes

IT must not be thought, then, that a mechanistic approach to lyricism was foreign to Horace or that such an approach on a critic's part would have outraged his soul. The whole of the *Ars Poetica* cries that message aloud. And as the setting off of A against B is the major motif of the Horatian verbal composition, so the search for applications of this technique of balance and contrast at the levels of phrase, stanza, and whole poem is the chief duty of the interpreter; whole poem, for the Odes are a corpus wherein the interrelation of units may possibly be as important as their own unity, and to understand one poem (however complete) at a time may be to understand less than the poet has achieved. Heinimann's perceptive remark about the poet's 'equilibrium of contrasts'[1] deserves a thorough exploitation, and this may be as instructively shown as anywhere in the published order of the odes—the order, that is to say, in which they present themselves to the reader in our text of the four books. The traditional arrangement is firmly based and only here and there are doubts sometimes aired about the position of particular odes; in the main it is not questioned that we have the poems in their original ordering[2] and that it was Horace who placed them so. It is right to ask, therefore, if there is not some design herein which is worth apprehending as such, and further, to what extent and in what way the ordering of the odes affects the reader's appreciation of the whole lyric

[1] *Mus. Helv.* 1952, 203.
[2] For the possibility of doubt, see F. Fontaine, 'Enchaînement et groupement des poèmes dans l'œuvre lyrique d'Horace', mémoire de licence, Liège, 1941–2, chap. i.

corpus—as it must do, whether contrived or fortuitous, in part or in entirety. Oddly enough, more answers have so far been given to the first of these questions: the second is more problematical, and more important in the long run; for to have poetry's impact defined only by poets' intentions (however optimistic) would make a dull world.

In this matter suspicion is the due of any analysis which claims to be other than tentative. If the eighty-eight odes of the first publication and the fifteen of the second were rearranged by being drawn out of a hat, it would not confound the critic to produce explanation and defence of the new result on artistic—or even cabalistic—grounds. And the second of our questions would still be valid. That theory will be best which admits that Horace himself might very well have produced a dozen different groupings on a dozen different days, and achieved much with each one: but this does not entitle us to alter the order to suit a theory or to widen the theory to fit any order.

It is of course reasonable to assume—indeed it would be surprising not to find—what may be called 'framework pegs', holding the corpus together in a somewhat external and preliminary fashion. Just as Virgil uses a symmetrical arrangement of rivets of this sort in the Georgics by calling upon his patron by name at i. 2, ii. 41, iii. 41, iv. 2, so Horace uses Maecenas likewise (to open one book, close another, and 'centre-pin' a third) at i. 1, ii. 20, and iii. 16. And the recognition of iv. 1 as an 'overture', quoting in advance many of the motifs of the book it opens, is equally reasonable and sound an observation.[1]

Wickham provided[2] several hints towards solving the first of our questions, and some of them are suggestive for the answer to the second. But they are hints of unequal value. It may be true that where odes are addressed in succession to

---

[1] Both observations are Fraenkel's, 229 f. and 413. It is to be noted, in view of what is said later, that i. 1 has three relationships of order: as 'overture' to Books I–III; as 'dedication' of Book I; and as one of the 'paraded' metrical essays, i. 1–9.

[2] Edn. of Horace, vol. (*Odes*)³, 1896, 25–30.

real and known persons they reflect Horace's mental association of, say, Pollio with Sallustius Crispus and Dellius (ii. 1, 2,
3); yet rather more tidiness would be expected than is found.
After all, to take this particular example, the very similar
admonition to Plancus is far away (i. 7), and even that to
Murena at some distance (ii. 10). And why should Pollio
call to mind people of so different a kind as Sallustius and
Dellius (for no comparison is pointed)? It is true again (to
take up a metrical point from the same scholar) that Horace
mostly avoids setting side by side odes in the same metre, and
this may preclude certain positionings; but, quite apart from
the exceptions, this consideration remains a negative one outside the so-called Parade Odes (i. 1–9), or outside the very
simple alternation of sapphics and alcaics in ii. 1–11.

Wickham also points to two movements of thought in
Horace: to the progress of poetic confidence discernible (from
irony, through uncertainty, to bold statement) in the first
three books (*quodsi me lyricis vatibus inseres* i. 1, *non usitata nec
tenui ferar penna* ii. 20, *exegi monumentum aere perennius* iii. 30);[1]
and to the ostensible development of political reflection in the
same collection of poems—and certainly a sense of deliverance,
characterizing the first book, does seem to give way to an
awareness of personal and social difficulties in the second, and
this in turn to a series of more or less plain recommendations
to emperor and people on the resolving of the moral crisis
(Book III). Because these are subjective analyses, they are not
the less credible: but neither does more than account for the
rough position of certain odes in relation to certain others,
building by separated 'points' a kind of 'average-temperature'
chart of the overall climate of thought in each book. But we
cannot speak of the 'time' and 'thought' of each book; the
published order of the poems is by no means their order of
composition, as some commentators have erroneously assumed.
A careful reading of the editions will make this clear.

But Wickham goes further: he remarks, with a glance at

[1] On the nature of Horace's claim in this ode, see Chap. III, pp. 69 f.

Horace's natural cast of mind, that irony is regularly and consciously employed expressly to prevent the political odes from bulking too large in the collection; and that Horace in fact carefully intersperses solemn with trivial. Thus mood as well as topic is taken into account by poet and by critic; and the latter now adduces the general principle of tone-contrast or 'change of key'. Personal odes are set beside public, banter beside earnestness, Stoicism beside Epicureanism. Unfortunately, the categories hardly match each other, having more to do in any case with elevation of style, and phraseology (and differences are easy to find between neighbouring odes); otherwise Wickham deserves praise for stressing Horace's modal or atmospheric achievement, so to speak, in poem-arrangement, which will be examined a little later; and here first appears an appeal to contrasts and oppositions articulating the whole collection.

It was the idea of a designed and meaningful pattern that appealed to Verrall, who evolved a detailed scheme of dating for the odes from the identification of apparent factual references within them.[1] With the aid of this time-scheme, he then sought to discover in Books I–III a historical progress of comment, hopes, and fears covering the period 40–20 B.C., and to reinforce this by citing a parallel series of seasonal references (winter—spring—summer—autumn—winter, etc.) in other odes which do not contain political allusions. Comment is perhaps superfluous on a thesis which has long ceased to convince. On either count, historical or seasonal, comparatively few odes are covered (five and nine respectively in Book I); and the seasonal backgrounds are themselves debatable.

Sturtevant's starting-point is the negative consideration already noted, that Horace tends to avoid repetition of the same metre in contiguous odes. As some explanation is called for when exceptions occur, it is suggested that the poems

---

[1] *Studies in Horace*, Essay III, 90–120. This theory is not quite dead: even recently the view has been quoted that an ode-date of 24–23 B.C. is 'too late' for Book I (see Dilke, *BICS*, 1958, 53).

concerned are connected in topic, and so override the poet's liking for metrical *variatio*. Now the number of odes interconnected by cross-reference of ideas, aphorisms, political and philosophical observations, *exempla*, and so on is a high one: in fact Horace's locutions far outnumber his ideas, and very few odes stand quite alone. Still, pointing to the obvious case of the Roman Odes, Sturtevant produces[1] an apologia for the 'oddity' of metrical sequence of i. 16 and 17 (Tyndaris); 34 and 35 (Fortune); ii. 13, 14, and 15 (death and misused wealth); iii. 24 and 25 (correction of pessimism); iv. 14 and 15 ('Augustan'). (ii. 19 and 20 is written off as an 'inevitable' juxtaposition, as if the latter ode could not be longer delayed or the former not put elsewhere, which reminds one of nothing so much as Dante's 'ma perchè piene son tutte le carte ordite a questa cantica seconda . . .'.) Once only a connexion (or rather an opposition) of mood is noted: the fervour of iii. 25 answers the gloom of its predecessor. Yet even here it is the factual relation which is stressed—that Augustus *was* doing all that could be desired to heal the sickness in public morals. Similarly, when help comes in the matter of i. 26 and 27—which Sturtevant frankly gives up—the topical relation is again put forward (that both have to do with a feast), although a truer binding element is the atmosphere of light-heartedness, not to say lightheadedness, which pervades them both.[2] And Sturtevant summarily dismisses, in favour of the overt reference to Fortuna, Kiessling's interesting remark that i. 34 appears to put the reader in the proper frame of mind for the ode which follows it.

So far, some artistic design has been allowed in the arrangement, but rarely as a pervasive impulse, or as other than a conscious act of the poet's. It is the first of our questions which

---

[1] *CR*, 1912, 119–22.

[2] Adelaide Hahn, *TAPA*, 1939, 225 and 226 n. 1: yet the feasts (or, in i. 26, projected feast) are said to be respectively characterized as restrained and brawling, or calm and angry—the reverse *modal* contrast to i. 16 and 17, with which 27 and 26 respectively have affinities of expression. If these particular oppositions do not leap to everyone's eye, the introduction of modal appreciation is very welcome. (Hahn also supports, with rhythmical evidence, Sturtevant's connexion of i. 16 and 17.)

is getting the answers. To be sure, relation of topic must be admitted as a factor in holding contiguous odes in groups—if one looks no further than the Roman Odes (placed together as they are by arrangement rather than commission, it would seem) :[1] and some credit must be given to the influence of metre—if one admits only the calculated differences of the Parade Odes and the alcaic–sapphic alternation of ii. 1–11. Now, as has been seen, repetition of topics and ideas is so integral a part of Horace's lyric method as to preclude its having special force in purposeful juxtaposing of individual poems. There are exceptions, for a repetition may be strengthened by close positioning, as to some extent again in the Roman Odes (yet the position of iii. 24, and even ii. 15, should be noted) ; or a contrast on this plane may have to be made while the reader's memory of a remark is fresh, like the antithesis of the unsuccessful and successful escape from hell at the close of, respectively, ii. 18 and 19 (yet one thinks of the actual quotation in iv. 9. 40 ff. of several odes published ten years before). What really happens, if Horace speaks of the same thing, more or less, in a close sequence of odes, is that the reader's mind is held in a certain receptive poise rather than in a fixed logical groove. Not that this has gone entirely unnoticed even in the Roman Odes : among recent critics one[2] defends the 'Roman', as opposed to personal, character of iii. 1, by appeal to its dignity and aloofness, its identity in cast of thought with the

---

[1] This is the consensus of opinion on a point which even Fraenkel's (260 ff.) convincing display of structural and meaningful connexion between poems in the 'cycle'—even organic connexion—leaves unsolved (see his n. 2 on p. 260). See the bibliographical remarks of Burck in Kiessling–Heinze's edn. i[8] (1955), 613 ff. A concentric arrangement is seen in *Odes* iii. 2–6 most recently by Perret, *Horace*, 107 (after Maury) ; and we are well reminded of the elements common to, for example, iii. 3 and iii. 5 (each ode appeals to myth or history, each contains a speech, each introduces the name Augustus). But parallelism of internal *structure* in these two odes, as described by Fraenkel (267), is hard to see : that 'in both the centre of interest lies in the weighty speeches' is true but really exhausts the correspondence. The Juno episode is Greek–Roman, the Regulus only Roman : and on the thought-plan of each ode, see pp. 89, 120. It is, however, much more convincing to say that these odes, both in a sense 'historical', frame the principal piece in the cycle, iii. 4.

[2] F. Solmsen, *AJP*, 1947, 337–52 (a most cogent paper).

next five odes; and another[1] would transfer ii. 15 (which, as Solmsen says of iii. 1, avoids the personal pronouns) to stand as the proem to iii. 6—which is at least to recognize that their air of shocked solemnity, occasioned by visible evidence of the materialism of the age, is the same. But on the whole this is not the prevalent view. Horace has usually been credited with nothing more than an occasional combination of ode with ode where the topic is alike[2] or the metre suggestively differentiated; and there has been a shift to even greater conservatism, as when it is said that the poet adopted 'any stray principle' in ordering the odes before publication, and that 'here and there odes are put next to one another for some common factor; thus i. 14 and 15 appear to be political allegories, i. 27 and 28 are dramatic monologues, i. 34 and 35 are both about Fortuna. Any idea, such as Verrall's, that the Odes are anything but a miscellaneous collection, is chimerical.'[3] In the face of this, a wary tread is called for.

Ingenuity can produce remarkable results, but also saddeningly shallow and excessively neat results, by employing the criterion of likeness of topic (with or without verbal reinforcement), or the twin criteria of like topic and balanced metre. A notable success is that of Fraenkel (419, 421 ff.), who sees a structural nucleus in Book IV (odes 7, 8, and 9). It is very likely indeed that Horace felt that the heterogeneous (and so much less subtle) fourth book—with personal poems, 'sparked off' by the *Carmen Saeculare* and belated fame as a lyricist, Augustan commissions, and reworkings of earlier ideas set cheek by jowl—that such a collection needed careful articulation. Hence the 'overture' iv. 1 (*Intermissa, Venus*); hence the junctions of iv. 4 and 5, iv. 14 and 15; and hence it may be that iv. 8 (*Donarem pateras*) is a centre-pin, itself carrying the most important fresh message of the book (in the poet's own eyes), namely that

---

[1] A. Y. Campbell, edn.[2] of *Odes and Epodes*, 1953 (ad loc.). See also Fontaine, op. cit.

[2] A topical schema was long ago suggested for the second book of the Satires (*abcd : abcd*) by Boll and Weinreich (*Hermes*, 1913, 143, and 1916, 412).

[3] Wilkinson, 15.

poetry has the power to confer immortality on those about whom it sings. Then this ode may well be flanked on this side by a preparation, iv. 7 (*Diffugere nives*), which declares the completeness of the annihilation of death (normally speaking); and on that by a corroboration, iv. 9 (*Ne forte credas interitura*), claiming for lyric (including Horace's own) a like power to that of epic and applying it to an individual's (Lollius') case. This analytical scheme has shortcomings (e.g. the message of iv. 8 was implied years before, in iii. 25. 5 f.; and from iv. 7 by itself one could not forecast the drift of the next ode—which may add to the impact of the Censorinus-ode, but sows seeds of doubt about such an interpretation of the collocation). But this is merely a result of separate composition; the arrangement is adroit.

Here the obvious metrical interplay of alcaics and sapphics at ii. 1–11 has attracted comment long since. The rough connexion of subject-matter of successive poems in the sequence has not gone unmarked, either. In the fullest recent treatment, by W. Ludwig,[1] the first twelve odes of the second book have their interrelation exalted into a highly contrived symmetrical structure of this sort:

1 to a patron and man of letters (Asinius Pollio)
  2 and 3 philosophic (to 'friends' of the emperor)
    4 and 5 erotic
      6 and 7 to Horace's own friends (adventure motif)
    8 and 9 erotic
  10 and 11 philosophic
12 to *the* patron (Maecenas).

The structural chiasmus is said by Ludwig to be revealed all

[1] *Hermes*, 1957, 336–45, based on Wilhelm Port's diagnosis of ii. 1–12 as 'metrisch und inhaltlich ein Ganzes' (*Philologus*, 1926, 299 f.). See also Kiessling–Heinze, i[8] (1955), 163, for whom ii. 2–11 and 13–20 are ordered by pairs. Fontaine (op. cit. 161–92) had anticipated Ludwig's scheme, but saw 'moderation' as the theme of ii. 1–3, 10–12, which is hard to accept for ii. 1 or ii. 12 (and would be perfectly easy for ii. 9). The scheme of J. Perret (*Horace*, 1959, 104 f.) is like Port–Ludwig's for ii. 2–11, and equally symmetrical for ii. 13–20 (13–14, 19–20 on the poet's relation to death, 15 and 18 against luxury, 16 of *otium*, and 17 of friendship); but ii. 19 has in fact quite another subject.

the more clearly by the special emphasis accorded to the verbal rivets which tie the pairs internally and externally together, especially 6 and 7;[1] and as this group of odes is both preceded and followed by 38 other odes in the first publication it is centrally placed in the corpus; while 6 and 7, which form the nucleus of the group itself, comprise the quintessence of the Horatian lyric—the σφραγίς, so to speak[2]—with the keyword *vatis* at their own centre.

The perceptive reader must perhaps steel himself against thinking how much less suitable and convincing such an arithmetical schema is for inter- as opposed to intra-ode connexion; indeed it is hard to conceive any poet arranging (not composing) anything so nicely balanced. It is not as if the two collections of odes were each an organic unity by definition and concept as was, shall we say, the *Aeneid*,[3] so that a close-knit scheme or complex of schemes must inevitably be presumed as the ground-plan of the whole. In a work of that sort the parts are meaningful only as parts, and to excerpt, as if they could be treated as wholes, is really to mislead (or, if the part has its own life and apparent autarky, like Dido's tragedy, it sets up an artistic problem of its own). But with Horace's

---

[1] See Chap. IV, p. 131.

[2] So Ludwig (345). But on the nature of such 'seals' see Wilamowitz, *Sappho und Simonides*, 296 ff. L. Woodbury sums it up thus (*Studies in honour of Gilbert Norwood* (1952), 29): 'in each case the seal consists of the name of the author and affirms that the object so sealed, whether motion or poem, is his.' Also, it must be at the end of the work (the place where, in a Roman book, it would at once catch the eye, as at Virg. *G* iv. 559–66). See also Fraenkel, 362 f. Even if the end of an individual ode were an admissible place for a σφραγίς, the expected formula is that of iv. 6. 44, *vatis Horati*, which Porphyrion, but not the manuscripts, know as a variant in ii. 6. 24. (On the reason why Horace inserted his name at the end of iv. 6, see Fraenkel, 406; as to the essential force of *amici* at the close of ii. 6, see Chap. IV, p. 131.)

[3] A similar concentric structure is proposed for the *Aeneid* by W. A. Camps, *CQ*, 1954, 214 f., and 1959, 53 ff. To deal in this way with extensive monometric sections which carry a complicated but unified plot is plausible for composer and interpreter alike; much less is this the case where the material is multifarious lyric. The purely arithmetical architecture seen in the *Eclogues* by Maury and Perret (English readers may for convenience be referred to Hardie's review at *JRS*, 1953, 221 f.) has no place in the Odes, even if ii. 1–12 all have either 24 or 28 verses or Book III is divisible into three groups of 336 verses each (Perret, *Horace*, 106; in fact the latter figures are 336, 332, 336).

lyric the parts do exist separately : they gain very much—more, indeed, than is usually allowed—from their relation to the whole and to other parts, contiguous or distant.

Still, the 'context' remains factitious, an important extra but not an essential; and Ludwig's (like Fraenkel's) type of analysis is valuable in so far as the effect *is* merely one of arrangement of complete and pre-existing units, which is why ii. 12 (asclepiadic) is metrically anomalous in the group without necessarily being foreign to it. And it is no drawback to this theory that ii. 6 and 7 show a vastly different internal structure of thought (see pp. 86, 145 ff.), or that *mecum* in 7. 1 looks backwards to *mecum* in 6. 1 in external order-relation and forwards to *tecum* in 7. 9 in internal thought-relation : elements operate simultaneously in different directions at different levels of appreciation, and the reader must and does synthesize them. Ludwig's notion reinforces the organizing effect of the very loose 'ring-structure' of Books I–III (i. 1 and iii. 29 are both addressed to Maecenas, descendant of kings) by establishing a 'core-structure', too. Furthermore, it displays an aesthetic contrast of masses, organized against unorganized, ii. 1–12 against the rest, in the collection as a whole.

The real objections are these : first, our second question is not adequately answered, since it needs to be shown that so overt and mechanical a scheme has an equally overt effect (for, unlike the structures of the individual odes, it is not a framework for composing), whereas it seems on the whole to have passed unnoticed by interpreters and readers : secondly, this procedure of analysis and its results are at variance in one important respect with Horace's method, for his undoubted use (on the same level) of more or less subtle cross-references of topic to corroborate, to deepen by association, or to correct his meaning demands topical relation in non-contiguous odes (so that ii. 7 needs memory not only of ii. 6, but of ii. 3 and even i. 36—even, to be sure, of the idea-pattern of i. 4 (see Chapter IV)). All this robs purely topical interplay in *successive* odes of much of its architectural as well as interpretative significance,

unless it is strikingly new or bold, as perhaps in iv. 8 and 9.
ii. 2 and 3 are allied as a pair rather with i. 7 and ii. 10 than
with ii. 10 and 11, for then we see a group of admonitory
addresses to public figures who deserved them. Metrically, too,
the mere succession of sapphic–alcaic is not hard to find elsewhere, with no special function (i. 25 and 26, 30 and 31, i. 38
and ii. 1, etc.). Emphasis on topic is excellent as far as it goes:[1]
we must simply go farther. What is necessary is to look for an
element of linkage which is not equally operable at a distance,
such that distant odes may share it without being welded together by it, and which transcends mere topical, verbal, and
metrical likeness or unlikeness, transcends in effect the visual
and acoustic dimensions of the individual ode, and can linger
after the poem ceases. This is best called *atmosphere*. It is an
element which itself shows an artistic relationship with the
other elements of linkage, but has its own quite separate
existence.

To see how atmosphere plays its part as an aesthetic factor in
this entire lyrical achievement of Horace's, it will be useful to
diagnose and state its significant occurrences just as in the case
of connexions of topic. Of the latter, Ludwig's example which
we have just seen was particularly luminous: but there are
other, short-range, employments of the device, that is, of
purely topical junction. It may be that an ode, in its beginning,
picks up the subject or situation of its predecessor before striking out on a fresh line of its own—so the desperate fight of the
allegorical ship of i. 14 is used as a 'lead-in' to the equally
desperate and equally allegorical voyage which is the scene
of the next poem, even if that scene is not mentioned or exploited after the opening stanza. No doubt *O matre pulchra filia
pulchrior* (i. 16. 1) would forge a mental link in the reader's
mind with Helen of the previous ode and Tyndaris (of all

---

[1] And provided it is credible; but one drawback of Ludwig's schema is that
ii. 9 is not simply 'erotic', nor is ii. 11 'philosophic' unless we are very broad-
minded about philosophy and swallow, in its name, not only the last three
hedonistic stanzas, but even what appears to be a direct injunction *not* to think
at all (*vv.* 11 f.).

names) of the following. In the case of i. 18 the whole poem has for its burden the dangers of *Liber immodicus*; to this the close of i. 17, with its characterization of Cyrus as one whose amorous proclivities are tiresomely stirred by wine, serves as a most suitable preface.[1] So does Lalage bring Chloe to mind (i. 22 and 23), or one group of lovers introduce another (iii. 19 and 20). The link may even be restricted to the close of the first and the opening of the second ode, a coupling of the simplest sort. In this way the young men who (metaphorically) toss dry leaves into the river, at the end of i. 25,[2] fade, with a cinematograph continuity, into the picture of Horace himself hurling sorrows and fears to the winds and waves (i. 26 init.); or the party we leave in full revel as i. 36 ends receives fresh impetus at the start of the Cleopatra ode (i. 37). Odes 1–3 of the third book scarcely admit of a pause between them (which may help to explain why Porphyrion, or Diomedes, thought of the Roman Odes as one):

> cur valle permutem Sabina
> divitias operosiores? —
> — angustam amice pauperiem pati

and

> raro antecedentem scelestum
> deseruit pede Poena claudo. —
> — iustum et tenacem propositi virum

—as if each ode ended with a μέν clause, to be picked up with an antithetical δέ clause in the next. And the Muse, reproached for the grandeur of her song at the close of iii. 3, is invited to embark on lengthy choric melody at the next ode's very outset.

This is the simplest connexion and the simplest variation;

---

[1] The frequent alliance of Bacchus and Venus in the Odes is quite unexceptionable, these being the deities who preside over the relaxation of inhibitions as do no others, save perhaps Cybele. Cf. Euripides, *Hipp.* and *Bacch. passim*, but esp. *Hipp.* 443, *Bacch.* 300; note also *Bacch.* 402 ff., with Dodds's commentary ad loc., for the literary, art, and cult connexions.

[2] Housman and now Klingner prefer the Aldine's *Euro* (for the same alternative to *Hebro*, cf. Virg. *Aen.* i. 317). *Hiemis sodali* is like *veris comites* (iv. 12. 1, of winds); but i. 16. 4 argues a watery receptacle for the unwanted. i. 26. 2 f. allows both winds and sea.

sometimes the odes do not immediately look to their neighbours (cf. iii. 5 and 6 with what has just been said) and
sometimes they do. The next step is to appreciate whole-ode
relationship of topic or setting. The fourth and fifth odes of Book
II are both entirely concerned with the giving of advice, by the
experienced Horace, to a troubled lover; the sixth and seventh
both represent Horace as a veteran of unpleasant overseas wars
addressing a comrade (or would-be comrade). ii. 13 and 14
are both about death and the underworld; iii. 22 and 23 treat
of rustic devotions; iv. 10 and 11 of lovers lukewarm, or less, to
the poet; and reflexions on poetic ability comprise iv. 2 and 3
alike, however different their tone and conclusions. To this
last pair the combination of iv. 8 and 9 is a sort of first cousin,
the theme of these odes being largely

> dignum laude virum Musa vetat mori.

Now it is true that something besides literary criticism is in iv.
2, and a recommendation of poetry as an immortalizing agent
is not all that occupies the later part of iv. 9: but these topics
bulk largest in their respective odes, and we shall see that a
divergence between ode-division and topic-division is a feature
which Horace has more than once.

A glance at iii. 9, 10, 11, and 12 will confirm that Horace
can sustain a general subject over a block of odes: each one
here has to do with some aspect of unattainable or interrupted
desire. Certainly they have their individual touches. The first
has a hopeful ending; the fourth is written from the young
lady's point of view; and while the heroine of 10 is *saevo nupta
viro*, she of 11 (that is, the protatic character, Lyde: let us for
the moment ignore Hypermestra's episode) is *nuptiarum expers
et adhuc protervo cruda marito*. Yet the topic is the same throughout, turned to display its varied facets.

Now is the time to apply the criterion of atmosphere: it is
very noticeable that each of these odes has an atmosphere of
its own, quite distinct from that of its neighbours; a modern
musical setting of each might reveal this best. So, on a smaller

scale, there is an observable difference between ii. 4 and 5, or, even more significantly, 6 and 7. In the first pair the words are those of an experienced man of the world: but the polite mockery of ii. 4 is then replaced in 5 by a bluntness or coarseness which lasts for several stanzas. And when Horace declines to be dragged off on an odyssey by Septimius his war-weariness, his urge to vegetate and quietly die, is only half-serious: but to Pompeius he is sincere, and nothing could ring truer than the air of bitter-sweet reminiscence and the relief he shares with his friend that the strife is now over.

Although a separate exploitation of atmosphere will appear later, it is in most cases true that a topic or setting carries a mood or atmosphere with it.[1] i. 2 and 3 are alike pervaded by an air of solemnity according well with their common elements of topic—man's moral impertinence and the gods' anger—and by a concomitant undertone of mockery, too. Quiet introspection fills i. 31 and 32 in which the poet addresses in formulae of prayer the god who is the patron of his art and the instrument which symbolizes it.[2] As he dilates, *gliscente adulatione*, on the warlike and civil achievements of Augustus in the two odes which close the whole collection, sense and mood are one. The repetitive positiveness of the first (note the eleven occurrences of 'te, tuos', etc., in iv. 14. 33–52) is the consequence of its being cast in hymnic form. Nor can one detect any real variation in either subject (the dangers of the alliance of Bacchus and Venus) or atmosphere (excess, violence, and emergency) in that block which begins at i. 17. 21 and does not end until the last verse of i. 19.[3]

Whereas, however, the maintenance of a (general) topic, whether it carries with it precisely the same mood throughout or not, is essentially a device to create a sense of continuity of

[1] An immediate example to the contrary is afforded by ii. 13 and 14. Both are about death; but the latter is uncompromisingly stern, while the former is only partly (*vv.* 13–20) philosophic in tone, and elsewhere frankly jocular or full of an ingenuous wonderment at the sights of the nether world.

[2] On the nature of i. 32, see Fraenkel, 168 ff.

[3] See Chap. IV, p. 128 n. 1.

reference between certain poems, a maintenance of mood for its own sake, with or without similarity of topic, has a somewhat different aim (or, at least, effect). The reader is set in a frame of mind in which he will better appreciate and be more deeply struck by the poet's next words. The episodes and choral songs of tragedy suggest a ready analogy.[1] Those that go before condition the audience, if a matter of fact is revealed, to wallow happily in dramatic irony or enjoy the thrill of horror, when, to take a simple example, Dionysus makes insolent play with the dress and hair of the prince who served him likewise some scenes earlier (Eur. *Bacchae* 493–7, 925– 44). But another possibility arises where the relevant utterances follow without a break; the playwright then organizes an especially receptive not to say vulnerable state of mind in the audience—and Sophocles does this repeatedly[2]—so as, for example, to drop the announcement of catastrophe into a mood of excited optimism. Or—as with Aesch. *Agam.* 1331 f.— a forewarning which is *not* falsified may heighten the drama. The effect of these juxtapositions is no longer factual and delayed, but modal and immediate. And although the Odes are not a drama and their part–whole relationship is so very different, it was open to Horace to secure (whether wittingly or not) at least something of this sharpening of poetic 'attack'.

It is not hard to cite the probable cases. i. 34 and 35 have already been mentioned; the plea for Caesar's safety and the cry *quid intactum nefasti liquimus?* strike home upon an already sober and apprehensive reader, with *valet ima summis mutare . . . deus* still ringing in his ears. The warning to the unpredictable adventurer Dellius (ii. 3) comes pat upon a finger-wagging address to another public figure who is exposed to temptation, just as ii. 9 (*pace* Port–Ludwig) leaves an aura of the majesty of the ruler of Rome lingering at the outset of a warning to one

----

[1] Thus Solmsen, *Hesiod and Aeschylus*, 193, says 'the choruses of *Agamemnon* put us in a frame of mind in which we are prepared to experience a reversal of the king's fortunes'.

[2] See Kitto, *Greek Tragedy*[2], 162 (his examples cover the *Ajax*, *Antigone*, and *Oedipus Tyrannus*).

who might, and did, challenge it. As with continuation of topic, so the carrying over of mood or atmosphere sometimes presents blocks of odes whose effect is one. The Roman Odes come here into their own : the second, and still more the diffuse fourth, would make singularly little modal impression in isolation (less by far, one would judge, than iii. 24). Together the group builds a climax of increasing contemporary national relevance, increasing forthrightness and indignation, increasing pessimism.

The corollary to this is the strong adversative relation of mood to mood—the Sophoclean touch. Dismay is sharpened by the joy of a moment before, crudeness gives a savage jolt to sentimentality, pleasure comes with double force after pain.[1] It is in this sense that one should take Sturtevant's observation on iii. 24 and 25, where the determined cheerfulness and Augustan fervour of the latter cut through the air of gloom and crisis of the former ode. Equally Horace brings the gentle fussiness and mundane considerations of i. 38 to bear upon the solemnity and sense of drama evoked by the tale of Cleopatra's fortitude. The continuation of mood has, then, this converse : its studied and swift dissipation. This means that iii. 7 is not— if anyone thought it was—the inept effusion of a relieved author now that the patriotic section of the work is closed.[2] Horace must set the first six odes of the book clearly apart and not allow their incisive quality to suffer a gradual blunting. After a crescendo like

> aetas parentum peior avis tulit
> nos nequiores, mox daturos
> progeniem vitiosiorem

[1] Or the reverse, as at iv. 1. 33.

[2] The 'mitte civilis super urbe curas' of the next ode would jar more. Or, to put it more fully, the complacent and thankful report of peace on all frontiers (iii. 8. 19 ff.; cf. iv. 5. 25 ff.) nullifies the *metus externus* which is used in iii. 6 (7 ff. and *passim*) to drive home the critical nature of the moral and religious collapse. But a poet attending to one point will often ignore or undermine another: cf. Virgil's 'facilem victum' (*G* ii. 460) with the rest of the *Georgics*; and, in the Odes, iii. 2. 25–29 with iii. 21. 14–16, or i. 3. 21–24 with iii. 3. 53–56. (Of course, Maecenas *has* worried about the state, unlike the castigated public: but we are concerned with the proximity of these odes.)

a line must be drawn, or a curtain lowered, and only something very different in atmosphere (and of course in subject and metre) will serve: *Quid fles Asterie . . .?* It is at least a striking suggestion that the ingrafted crudity of *S* i. 5. 84 ff. owes its place not simply to its Lucilian origin but to hide Horace's emotional response to the first sight on that journey to Brundisium of the hills of his native Apulia.[1] No doubt a similar and perhaps instinctive desire to cut clean away from a passage of sentiment and sorrow before it degenerates into sentimentality and mere tearfulness—no doubt such is the motivation for following the moving reflections on Quintilius' death (i. 24) with the shock of *Parcius iunctas quatiunt fenestras . . .*, the crudest and nastiest poem in Horace's lyrics.[2] It is safe enough to believe that positioning of this sort cannot be due to some accident which escaped the notice of a preoccupied poet at the moment of editing; it is in any case the same device that operates inside an ode (in reverse fashion) at i. 10. 9–12 and 13–16, the touching and dignified episode of Priam's mission neutralizing the frankly comic outwitting of Apollo.[3] Horace may fairly be credited with some design in ordering the odes as he did. Besides, it is a material point that the nature of a contemporary *volumen* prevented any reader turning to any ode (even after he had learnt his way about the collection) except by way of its neighbours (on one side or the other) in order.

The texture of this body of lyric is made up, then, of manifold oppositions of whole poems. There is one between the significant (artistically speaking) and the much more frequent insignificant juxtaposing of odes, for it is folly to think that even most of the odes are grouped according to some masterplan; there is another between the continuation of a mood and its dissipation; yet another between the continuation of

[1] Alfred Noyes, *Portrait of Horace*, 81 (and cf. Fraenkel, 416, on the end of iv. 13).

[2] But not without wit: the only hugging at Lydia's house will be between door and threshold (3 f.); and the Thracian wind (Boreas) acts as uncontrollably as all Thracians (*bacchante*, 11).

[3] Just as the relation of iii. 6 to iii. 7 is very much that of the parts of iii. 14 to each other.

a mood or atmosphere and the continuation of topic or factual references or setting. It is important to appreciate, too, a further tension between those places where topic and mood go hand-in-hand, or at least do not positively offset each other, and the rarer occasions when these elements are themselves set in noticeable contrast.¹ We have seen already how the sequence iii. 9, 10, 11, 12 is a block by the criterion of similar general subject, but a scatter of small-scale contrasts in atmosphere, personal types, degree of sophistication. Conversely the Roman Odes deploy like, but not at all identical, ideas; yet their mood is uniform. Two more such sequences offer themselves as evidence here. The ninth, tenth, and eleventh odes of Book II are all admonitory, but they ally themselves in spirit and not in particularities. In each case Horace is trying to break through the melancholy or fretfulness of an acquaintance, and to assure him that the crisis is not worth his tears, that the present state of affairs will not be for ever. Horace's own manner is all the time one of determined altruistic cheerfulness, his air that of an extravert ministering to the inward-looking. But the content of his advice is very varied. Valgius' trouble is a poet's lachrymose preoccupation with the *molles querelae* of the heart—he is to be diverted to nobler, or grander, themes: Murena² is obsessed in particular with the restrictions of his present life (now that adventurers are at a discount)—he is to be told that the darkest hour is before the dawn and the middle road is the safest, pitifully inadequate clichés as they are: Hirpinus is merely a too-solemn young man, excessively beset

¹ E. T. Silk, *AJP*, 1956, 255 ff. regards ii. 18, 19, and 20 (following Wili, *Horaz*, 233, he gives them the common theme of 'victory over death') as forming at once a climax and an antithesis to the rest of Book II: furthermore he would see in ii. 20 an 'overture' to the Roman Odes, and in the Dionysiac ii. 19 a 'prologue' to the block ii. 20–iii. 6 (as the Dionysiac iii. 25 is an 'epilogue' to iii. 24). There is almost nothing acceptable in all this. ii. 18 is not about victory over death, but about death's victory over the unfair advantages (in life) of the rich; ii. 20 has only one phrase relevant to the Roman Odes (*vv.* 1–3), and that is said, anyway, at iii. 1. 2–4; 'prologue' and 'epilogue' are too loosely applied to mean much; and this theory raises the most complex problems of topic and mood relationship.
² On the identification of this addressee, see Chap. III, p. 70, n. 2.

with political anxieties—he needs a drink, a song, and a girl's company. So goes the studied maintenance of atmosphere and the variation of topical detail.[1]

Precisely the opposite pattern of structure is visible in iii. 19, 20, and 21. The drinking party of the first of these odes ends with all attention turned to love-making: the next discourses further on the perils of amorous entanglements: the third returns to the delights of the wine-jar and its patron deity and (with that very common combination of divinities) *si laeta aderit, Venus*. But the mental climate of each poem is highly individual. The reader is invited to pass from the hearty and heated and naïve banqueters and their *demens strepitus* to the cold, sophisticated scene with Nearchus at its centre, embodying the careless cruelty of one *qui se laisse aimer*; and thence to resort to the dusty but more humane air of a scholar's study, where a jar is unsealed and a learned parody worked out with equal care and regard for tradition, and where the conversation is almost visibly proceeding with learned footnotes (cf. *vv.* 11–12).

Thus the Odes appear to rely to a notable extent on the reader's mental associations and prevailing frame of mind alike, and even to do much to control, as well as exploit, them both. Of course, it must be said once again that it is idle to pretend that the entire corpus is organized systematically to that end. It would be as foolish, in a later chapter, to see a highly complex scheme of ideas in every ode. In either case there is a great mass of neutral material; if it were not so, the result would be aesthetic indigestion for the reader. This needs to be admitted, because the common coincidence of shift of topic

---

[1] I should not be unduly ruffled to find another critic proclaiming that this block has like topic (Horace's advice to the puzzled) but varied atmospheres (matching the diverse personalities of Valgius, Murena, and Hirpinus). At least this would recognize the essential point—a contrast or tension of some kind. But in fact such an analysis would be stating the topic only very generally and ignoring the fact that Horace is throughout 'calling the tune' in the matter of mood, itself evoked by the similar imagery: *non semper imbres . . . manant—non, si male nunc, et olim sic erit*—(and subtly different) *non semper idem floribus est honor vernis*.

and mood with the break between odes, and the comparative rarity of Horace's maintaining theme and atmosphere from a point within one ode to a point within another (apart from the simplest end-and-start coupling), are strong arguments against the idea that 'disunity'—that is, indulging in 'block'-composition at the expense of the lineaments and formal identity of individual poems—is to be regarded as an essential feature of Augustan poetry. That position is too extreme. All that is necessary, towards answering both the questions we asked at the outset, is to appreciate that there is a little more complexity than is generally recognized in the arrangement of the completed odes by their author, and that we are presented with something more than a mere, if undeniable, succession of the political and the amorous, the grave and the gay.[1]

[1] Only after this chapter was written was a copy of the essay of F. Fontaine ('Enchaînement et groupement des poèmes dans l'œuvre lyrique d'Horace', mém. de licence, Liège, 1941–2) put into my hands, and this by the kindness of the author. This thesis suffers from the excess of zeal which would evolve a consistent theory of ordering to include all the odes; and despite references to 'ton' it really ignores atmosphere. But, however unconvinced one may be by the topical analysis offered for particular odes, or by the arithmetical arguments, it is encouraging to find set in opposition the principles of 'passage du même au même' and 'rupture de ton' (e.g., respectively, iii. 10, 11, and 12 succeeding to iii. 7, 8, and 9: 239 f.). And Fontaine (299 f.) already has much of Fraenkel's interpretation of the junction of iv. 7, 8, and 9 (see above, p. 42 f.). Any future essayist on this theme will do ill to ignore this treatment.

III

Contrast-technique 2: Thought-structure within the Odes

THE aesthetic achievement of placing whole poems in different external arrangements is a limited one, and to a large extent resides in the reader's cast of thought when all is done. At the other end of the scale, a poet's play with words and phrases and images produces effects of sense and sound as innumerable as striking, and the result is palpably more objective. The architecture of the individual odes in Horace lies between these extremes; it is moderately complex and moderately susceptible to critical analysis. Within one ode is found neither variety of metre nor variety in the elevation of the language; but in terms of thought and mood odes are built on designs which are themselves artistically satisfying. Here appreciation is entirely concerned with the content, that is, the meaning of each ode. The 'blocks' of sense,[1] extracted by examination of the meaning, stand in a structural relationship one to another in each ode.

The source of this use of blocks of thought (especially where there appears the additional element of responsion) is ostensibly the formal choir-lyric which in Greece stood in contrast to the personal melic genre; the latter fitted a cursive progress of the sense to the more direct expression of an individual's mental odyssey.[2] Pindar, for instance, is in the tradition of choral ode

---

[1] Cf. R. Reitzenstein, *Neue Jahrbücher*, xxi (1908), 102. We are not here concerned with the extension of the idea of 'blocks' (up to the point of denying all importance to divisions between poems) by E. Howald (see Chap. IV, p. 128, n. 1).

[2] See Bowra, *Greek Lyric Poetry*², 1 ff., and *New Chapters in Greek Literature*, iii. 2 ff. (optimistically quoting Horace *C* i. 1. 34 f. as making the distinction between the types; one might rather point to *lyra* . . . *tibia* at i. 12. 1 f., for that

composition, while Horace inherits the method and mental atmosphere of the melic poets, especially the Lesbians. But Horace's dependence on the more formal genre is equally evident, and goes beyond mere genuflexion to Pindar in particular as 'il miglior fabbro'. Besides, all lyric poets show a mixture of formality and informality in structure, and the Horatian odes may fairly be expected at the outset to show both a free-running non-responsive personal style and a block-built responsive 'public' style—and indeed a conflation of the two. But the responsive mode in Horace is not the same thing as in Pindar; and his combined mode is equally peculiar to him. For example, it is clear that when, as with Pindar, a strong large-scale verse pattern is the norm the innovation resides in the progressive and informal development of the thought, while for Horace it lies in the imposition of a *stricter* sense pattern; and the resulting mixtures are not alike.

It is time to define the terms which will be applied in what follows to the different modes of thought-expression. Where this expression contains utterances which balance one another and are incomplete in themselves (so that their joint existence forms one rounded idea) it is said to be *strophic*,[1] and is akin to the choral expressions in Greek tragedy at their most formal stage. A strophic form may be the whole ode or a part of it, and may have a progress of sense within it (cf. the climactic movement of Aesch. *Prom.* 887 ff., below) or be part of some

ode above all sees the marriage of the εἴδη). But a caveat (as to the modernity of this distinction) is given by A. E. Harvey, *CQ*, 1955, 159, n. 3 (but see 173, n. 4). The necessary difference of thought-structures inherent in this subdivision of lyric (whether 'official' or not) is well exploited by H. L. Tracy, *Studies in honour of Gilbert Norwood*, 203 ff.

[1] A strophic section which moves in a series of equivalent sense-units is *monostrophic* (and most nearly approaches the stanza-form of Lesbian and later melic); a balance by pairs (strophe, antistrophe) is *distrophic*; and the addition of a single section (epode) to a pair produces *triadic* sense-design. The epode of a metrical triad is metrically distinct in verse-patterning: the epode of a sense-triad is usually distinct in length. The term *antistrophic* (used by some to mean the same as our 'strophic') is here restricted to reference to the second member of a balanced pair of sections, as *epodic* refers only to the third in a triad. The repetitive *metrical* unit of, for example, four sapphic or four alcaic verses is uniformly called here a 'stanza', as is the regular English practice.

larger progress: but of itself it is the negation of progress, and the thought turns round upon itself. Add to strophic form careful features of repetition and relative length, and the expression may be seen to be *symmetrical*, or, if such features are only loosely employed, *patterned*. These modes have in common the element of *responsion*; expressions which are devoid of this characteristic complementary technique may or may not show progress of thought: but the opposition of *static* to *progressive* thought is strictly on another level of analysis, and responsive modes may also be static (i. 19) or progressive (iii. 9) in their total effect. In fact this second opposition is an alternative weapon in Horace's armoury of contrast devices.

iii. 9 offers a simple and precise example. This is a variant of the *carmen amoebaeum*, wherein the lovers match reproach with reproach and sigh with sigh in four-verse strophes and antistrophes:

> Donec gratus eram tibi
> nec quisquam potior bracchia candidae
>   cervici iuvenis dabat,
> Persarum vigui rege beatior.
>
> Donec non alia magis
> arsisti neque erat Lydia post Chloen,
>   multi Lydia nominis
> Romana vigui clarior Ilia, etc.

There are three such exchanges, in which the word echoes (*pro qua non metuam mori, si parcent animae fata superstiti—pro quo bis patiar mori, si parcent puero fata superstiti*) have a dual role. Of course they are 'psychological', for Lydia restricts herself to verbal mockery as long as the other has nothing positive to offer, but drops this at once when a reconciliation is in the wind, and takes the sting from her uncompromising shifting of the blame (and from her claim to be giving up a good thing) by a very pretty acceptance of the *status quo ante bellum* at the end. For all its mathematical precision of design this ode has a plot and (perhaps, for the ingenuous) a surprise. But the echoes also underline the strophic responsion of the ideas, and make the structure all the easier to grasp: those who are happier with formulae can write down something like *a1a2/b1b2/c1c2/* or *str.1 ant. 1/str. 2 ant. 2/str. 3 ant. 3.*[1]

Now at this point two objections may be raised. First, it may be asked whether Horace has not here taken over a well-known poetic form of which the balance and antithesis are integral, and done so once only—for there is nothing else in the collection quite like this (antiphonal singing in the centre of i. 21 is unlikely, and there is nothing like Catullus lxii, not even *Carmen Saeculare*), and strict pattern of this sort may well be very exceptional. This will be answered when the other odes discussed and analysed below are compared with iii. 9: none will be found to be identical with it in structure, but many will exhibit a similar patterning of parts of the thought, without any underlying inherited scheme peculiar to the type of ode. The second question is more radical: have we here anything different from the quantitative responsion of choral lyric, modified of course to fit the shorter metrical scheme of personal poetry? Certainly the metrical unit appears to be the distich, but there is evidence for crediting Horace with a four-verse stanza in this type of metre;[2] if this is sound, have we in iii. 9

[1] Although editors compare Theocritean and Virgilian examples, the poem nearest to this in spirit and in size of pattern, so to speak, is Catullus xlv (which has strophe, antistrophe, and epode, punctuated by ephymnia). iii. 9, it should be noted, answers its own balancing of like words and phrases with a subtle threefold variation-scheme. There is the 'capping' *variatio*, normal in this type of poem—e.g. *Persarum rege . . . Romana Ilia* and *non metuam mori . . . bis patiar mori*; secondly, there is the psychological *variatio* in the careful and face-saving insertion of 'face mutua' by the girl, or the way in which she ceases, when reconciliation is foreshadowed in this sad estrangement, to pick up her lover's exact wording (*donec . . . donec, me . . . me*, etc., but *quid si . . .? . . . quamquam . . .*; and so str. 3/ant. 3 are quite distinct from the preceding pairs); and thirdly, we see the purely artistic *variatio* which, in the one verse which could have been repeated exactly, replaces *animae* with *puero* (unless this is a dig at Horace), and which indulges in the extremely neat verbal shift of the last verse, *tecum vivere amem, tecum obeam libens*. (One should in fairness note, though, that if *reiectaeque* is correct in *v.* 20 Horace is ready to take the blame for the quarrel, despite his opening remark. And he is always complimentary (*candidae cervici*)—as is Lydia, too (*multi nominis* is a tribute to the power of her lover's poetry); and she would die *for* Calais but *with* Horace.)

[2] There is a theory that Horace always composed his lyrics in stanzas of four verses (the *Lex Meinekiana*), and many editors, following the lead of

anything other than strophic design still based firmly on metrical divisions?

This can only be answered by making clearer the essential differences between the two lyrical genres at their widest divergence; analysis of Horatian thought-structure depends on the recognition that with him metrical divisions (i.e. the pauses before repetitions of metrical sections, each identical with the preceding section) are in themselves quite irrelevant to the deployment of the sense. These divisions are convenient as

Vollmer, print accordingly. But Lenchantin de Gubernatis disagrees (*Athen.* 1944–5, 72 ff.), and the theory is accepted by Büchner only for the later odes (*Sitz. Leipzig. Akad.* 1939, 2, 38 ff.). iv. 8 alone presents an obvious problem, having a total number of verses not divisible by four. This has led to some extraordinary tinkering with that ode (although Peerlkamp's deletion of *vv.* 14–17, recently approved as if beyond argument by Maas, *Textual Criticism*, 34 f., has quite another basis and leaves this whole problem as it was, and wider considerations underlie the most recent 'solution', the excision of 15b–19a, 28, and 33, of C. Becker, *Hermes*, 1959, 212 ff.).

It is essential to regard the question of stanzas as a metrical problem in the first instance, and to solve it by purely metrical criteria (e.g. hiatus, synaphea, *syllaba anceps*: cf. Postgate, *CR*, 1918, 23 ff.) and without recourse to thought-features (e.g. transitions, antitheses, verbal anaphora). These latter can only determine thought-structure. When the two criteria have been *successively* applied with positive results, the situation will be everywhere found to be as in the obviously stanzaic odes (sapphics, alcaics, four-verse asclepiadic combinations like i. 5 or i. 15)—that is, with interplay between congruent and non-congruent verse- and thought-construction. (In passing, it would seem that Postgate's finding—that distichal metres tend to four-verse metrical blocks and monostichal metres (like iv. 8, to be sure) to two-verse blocks—is borne out at least in part by certain sense-structure elements: see p. 101.) By the two tests, of metre and of content, i. 13 shows four-verse stanzas plus four-verse sense-strophes. iii. 9 and i. 19 have four-verse stanzas plus four-verse distrophic sections. iii. 28 probably has four-verse stanzas (note the hiatus between *vv.* 4 and 5) but eight-verse strophe and antistrophe (1–8 on the wine, 9–16 on the songs) with no sense-break at 4/5 and no sense-break or even grammar-break at 12/13 (and so correct Fraenkel, 418, n. 3). iii. 30 has no metrical signs of four-verse structure (on the contrary, note the *syllabae ancipites* at the end of *vv.* 4 and 10 alike) but has perhaps the distichal trend Postgate saw in monostichal metres; yet in sense it shows an uneven three-part progression (1–5, 6–9, 10–14) plus a coda (14–16), on all of which see pp. 69 f. iv. 1 has hiatus at 16/17 and 20/21, but also at 18/19, suggesting (despite Postgate) distichal stanzas; but the thought-structure is far more complex (see pp. 81 f.). This whole problem needs a fresh and thorough review, in the first place under the two separate headings of metre and sense. (The insistence on *grammar*-breaks at the ends of all stanzas, against the sense-structure, is seen especially in iv. 12: cf. Melinno's hymn to Rome and Statius, *Silvae* iv. 7 (and Bowra, *JRS*, 1957, 22).)

boundary marks, and in practice sense-breaks and stanza-divisions usually fall together: but the sapphic stanza, for instance, is basically not a unit of sense.

Although in the first place the pattern of formal choral verse is determined by the movements of the dance or the repetition of the tune, to this the thought is soon related, so that a triad of verse arrangements (strophe, antistrophe, and epode) is matched by the statement, antithesis, and resolution (or extension) of the ideas.[1] Exactly so, in the fourth choral song of the *Prometheus Vinctus* (887 ff.), the Oceanids balance a wise man's pronouncement on the social foolishness of marrying out of one's class (str.) with a more personal and very natural disavowal of any desire for a divine bridegroom (in view of Io's fate) (ant.): then the song is rounded off by a quite distraught cry of immediate alarm in case they cannot avoid Zeus' amorous eye (ep.). It would be only natural that in certain cases (especially when extended narration was involved) the thought should flood over the strophic boundaries. Then two possibilities existed, strict strophic responsion of metre and thought—or at least the retention of self-contained strophes—or a sense-movement which ignored the metrical divisions. The second type creates a conflict between metrical and mental expression which plays an important part in the 'tempering' of the poem: and the poet can use it as a variation of texture alongside passages which show no such conflict.

All this is visible in the stasima of Aeschylus' tragedies. The fourth song of the chorus in the *Agamemnon* (975–1032) has strict responsion of both verse and sense; the first distrophic group dwells on foreboding of disaster (organized with a neat

---

[1] For the relation to dance or tune, see W. Kranz, *Stasimon*, 115. Metrical distrophism is probably Alcman's invention, but triadic arrangement is not seen so early. It is perhaps first found in [Ibycus] fr. 3 D (surely not really by Ibycus?—see A. E. Harvey, *CQ*, 1957, 222 f.). The exact relevance of Suidas' οὐδὲ τὰ τρία Στησιχόρου γινώσκεις has been debated since Crusius first referred it to the Palinode; yet one would expect this acme of formality in structure (i.e. triadic verse) in Stesichorus, if only to offset the long, continuous narrative. The history of strophic design is obscure; its presence in formal lyric visible to all.

antithesis between the long-past departure and the present
return of the fleet, chiastically arranged to end the strophe and
begin the antistrophe) : the second group contrasts the possibility of recuperation from ordinary ills with the impotence
of man to undo bloodshed. The whole forms a complex but
single idea. Contrast with this the third and fourth groups of
the preceding stasimon (738–81) ; across the division between
the two groups runs a reflection on the offspring of Good Deeds
and of Bad, and the antitheton ignores a strong natural pause :

$$. \quad . \quad . \quad \quad . \quad \quad . \quad . \qquad \qquad [ἀντ. γ$$
$$οἴκων \ γὰρ \ εὐθυδίκων$$
$$καλλίπαις \ πότμος \ αἰεί.$$

$$φιλεῖ \ δὲ \ τίκτειν, \ ὕβρις \ μὲν \ παλαι- \qquad \qquad [στρ. δ$$
$$\quad ὰ \ νεάζουσαν \ ἐν \ κακοῖς \ βροτῶν$$
$$ὕβριν \ . . .$$

(761–5 : the colometry is Fraenkel's.)

And when the description of events excites the thought,
metre and sense are equally commonly in conflict and in har-
mony. The satisfying texture of *Agam.* 104–257 is woven from
both effects.[1]

The Attic tragedians were subject, of course, to the contrary
pressures of competitive individualism and religious conservatism, so that while there intrude notable innovations and de-
partures from the early organization of lyric passages, neither
Sophocles nor Euripides finally discarded strophic form; in
the *Bacchae* Euripides returns both to an earlier atmosphere
of ideas and to an old-fashioned insistence on responsion of

---

[1] At 121, 139, 159 the refrain αἴλινον αἴλινον εἰπέ κτλ. stresses the responsion :
by the end of the fifth antistrophe metrical considerations are overridden in the
rising excitement :

$$στόματός \qquad \qquad [ἀντ. ε$$
$$τε \ καλλιπρῴρου \ φυλακᾷ \ κατασχεῖν$$
$$φθόγγον \ ἀραῖον \ οἴκοις$$
$$βίᾳ \ χαλινῶν \ τ' \ ἀναύδῳ \ μένει. \qquad \qquad [στρ. ζ$$
$$(235-8)$$

The effect of this variation is upon the reader's or hearer's sense of pattern or
form, and it combines with (but is other than) the effect which the differentia-
tion of mood within the ode has upon his emotional reflexes.

thought as well as metre in the stasima. The same combination of strict and free enlivens the 'public' lyric of Pindar and Bacchylides, whose myths are regularly constructed without parallel movement of verse and sense; and the larger range of possibilities is drawn upon with notable success, as for example (at a late stage of the poet's development) within and between the triads of the eighth Pythian.[1]

The Greek monodists and their successors had to work in the opposite direction. Not that Sappho or Alcaeus was conscious of a dichotomy in lyric poetry; the convenient division into choric and melic used by modern critics perhaps concerned only the festival organizer in antiquity.[2] But in practice the poets of the 'Dorian' choral style retained for the most part longer metrical units, where the Lesbians pushed the monostrophic form to its logical conclusion, under the influence, one supposes, of popular songs with their repetitions of tunes: that is, to stanzas of no great length and divisible into verses built on fixed alternation of long and short syllables.[3] These small-scale repetitive units encourage a separate movement of the ideas; otherwise a staccato and disjointed effect would be the rule. Still, the impulse to formal arrangement of the thought may have come from the choral writers, and Sappho at least is by no means artless in this respect. There is a blend of formal and informal in fr. 27 D, 16 L–P, where sense and phrasing link the first and fifth stanzas, between which runs a train of thought (Helen–Aphrodite–Anactoria) of the most cursive

---

[1] Cf. Euripides, *Hecuba* 905 ff. And in Horace's simile (iv. 2. 5 ff.) Pindar's style is said to overflow natural boundaries like a river in spate.

[2] Although Plato's reference (*Laws* 764d–e) is to an ideal community. Poets kept, in practice, to one or other side of the line between these types (so Sappho, Alcaeus, Anacreon range themselves against Stesichorus, Ibycus, Simonides, Pindar, Bacchylides). But the division is largely impressionistic, and in metre the length of responsive units, in content the emphasis often decides the matter. For example, Sappho fr. 27 D, 16 L–P contains the three traditional elements of choral lyric (myth, maxim, and personal reference) and is yet thoroughly private and monodic. See also Norwood, *Pindar*, 81 and n. 41. (There was no reason why Horace should not work towards Pindar, in, say, metrical effects: so C. W. Whitaker, *CQ*, 1956, 221 ff.)

[3] Cf. Lobel, Σαπφοῦς Μέλη, xxvi f. From Lesbos this type of verse passed to Anacreon.

kind.¹ The celebrated appeal to Aphrodite (fr. 1 D, L–P) looks
very like a triad of ideas: for three stanzas the poet speaks and
the goddess is in the limelight (first, possibly distant and hostile,
then credited with timely aid in the past, and, finally, pictured
as a swiftly descending avenger): for three antistrophic stanzas
Sappho's own woes are in the foreground but it is Aphrodite
who asks sympathetically about the trouble, hints of a change
for the better by her own intervention, and then describes the
thoroughness with which the situation will be reversed. An
epodic stanza joins the two movements of divine intervention
and human release, and completes the fusing with the keyword
σύμμαχος.² This is not a clear-cut design, and there is verbal
overflow where Horace would usually avoid it; but a pattern
emerges.

Horace's verse is varied enough: he has single- and double-
verse metres, quatrains, and once the (as editors print it)
multi-verse ionic decameter (iii. 12). But these are the small-
scale melic units, which cannot dominate or determine the
scheme of ideas, except in so far as the verse-divisions offer
punctuation-points for the sense. The pattern is of ideas alone,
expressed in comparable blocks of verses or stanzas: the ideas
alone give 'triadic' or 'distrophic' form. If the second ode of
Horace's first book (*Iam satis terris*) affords a good example of
a contrived thought-pattern, this is because the problem facing
the city is stated in two separate stanza-groups (each of three

¹ Most critics believe this to be the whole poem, although Page points to the
absence of positive indication that it is (*Sappho and Alcaeus*, 11, 55); cf. T. L.
Agar, *CR*, 1914, 190. Fr. 2 D, 31 L–P, is clearly incomplete but looks to have
a two-stanza thought-movement (*vv.* 1–8 give the situation—cf. Page, l.c. 26—
and Sappho's reaction (man–girl–self); 9–16 dwell on physiological details;
17 ff. strike a note of resignation, it would seem).
² This analysis of structure is not affected, as such, either by Page's idea (l.c.
12 ff.) that Sappho is wide-awake to her own fickleness and putting criticism
and reluctance to intervene into Aphrodite's mouth (reading κωὔ σε θέλοισαν.,
as Knox, in *v.* 24); or by Beattie's proposal (*CQ*, 1957, 182 f.) to place a stop
after φιλήσει and continue κῶς σὺ θέλοισα κτλ., which removes all positive
evidence of homosexuality from the poem and gives a regular hymnic use to
the participle (cf. also Fraenkel *ad* Aesch. *Agam.* 664)—although then a slight
blurring of strophic division is to be seen not only at *vv.* 12/13 but also at
24/25. (But see Gomme, *JHS*, 1957, 264, on the linguistic arguments.)

stanzas) in the first part of the poem, and the successful search for a present saviour is pursued in the second part in precisely balancing fashion.[1] A different arrangement of the sense would disrupt this ground-plan. Where the metre is a sort of a sleeping partner (at this level of analysis), the sections of sense are quite apt to show variations of their own in relative length or grouping. Horace's responsive composition is thus more complex than mere strophic design. It is also susceptible to outer contrasts: in fact, in place of a 'Pindaric' interplay between matched and divergent rhythm and sense, criticism of the Horatian lyric can recognize two possible basic oppositions:

(*a*) between responsive and non-responsive deployment of the thought,

and

(*b*) between different types of responsive arrangement, *or* (where that is absent) between static and progressive thought.

These contrasts help to set off one ode against another; they also spring upon the unwary within one and the same ode, and produce those dichotomies and apparent negations of unity (beloved word) which have exercised critics so much.[2] With this in mind, one can be more satisfied with i. 9 as a poetic creation—for to a careless reader the evocative setting and phraseology blur the objective presentation of situation and advice and the succinct use of the first contrast noted above. First comes a close triadic formulation of the ideas, opposing the cold and stiffness and strain (*laborantes*) of wintry nature outside to the warmth and relaxation produced by human efforts indoors (the snow is packed on the mountain but the

---

[1] So Tracy, *Studies in honour of Gilbert Norwood*, 209.

[2] For example, F. Heinimann, 'Die Einheit der horazischen Ode', *Mus. Helv.* 1952, 193 ff. Add to the critics quoted there Helen C. Toll, 'Unity in the Odes of Horace', *Phoenix*, 1955, 153 ff., who stresses contrasts of mood within single odes.

chill is dissolved by the fire; the wine flows if the rivers do not):

vides ut alta stet nive candidum   ('str.')
Soracte, nec iam sustineant onus
silvae laborantes, geluque
flumina constiterint acuto.

dissolve frigus ligna super foco   ('ant.')
large reponens atque benignius
deprome quadrimum Sabina,
o Thaliarche, merum diota:

and letting the two themes meet in a suggestion about human acceptance of life, underlined by reference again to the natural world:

permitte divis cetera, qui simul   ('ep.')
stravere ventos aequore fervido
deproeliantis, nec cupressi
nec veteres agitantur orni.

But the last three stanzas are nothing more than an informal and progressive train of thought, which starts from the cue *permitte divis cetera* but has its own course and its own plot, focusing more and more sharply upon one corner of an evening scene, and gradually forgetting philosophy in the preoccupation of one boy and one girl with each other:

quid sit futurum cras fuge quaerere et
quem Fors dierum cumque dabit lucro
appone, nec dulcis amores
sperne puer neque tu choreas,

donec virenti canities abest
morosa. nunc et campus et areae
lenesque sub noctem susurri
composita repetantur hora,

nunc et latentis proditor intimo
gratus puellae risus ab angulo
pignusque dereptum lacertis
aut digito male pertinaci.

None the less the two halves of the poem are welded by the

associative, indeed ambiguous, phrase *donec virenti canities abest*, while their opposition is ensured by the pervasive atmospheres, first of winter, then (by suggestion rather than overtly) of summer or warm spring.

Now to call this diptychal structure 'incongruous', or to say 'the end of the ode is not compatible with the beginning' (Fraenkel, 177 and n. 1), is quite misguided. Nor is it safe to quote the maxim 'denique sit quodvis, simplex dumtaxat et unum' (*AP* 23) as a Horatian abnegation of any degree of structural complexity; (on the limited critical value of the *Ars Poetica*, which sometimes accords with the practice of the Odes and sometimes does not, see Wilkinson's instructive remarks, 95 ff.; also Chapter I above, p. 20, n. 1). After all, there is nothing implausible in a man's declaring on a winter's day that summer evenings should not be wasted, and dwelling on their delights. In any case, this ode is an artistic essay in form, with two strongly contrasting, but linked sections: if equivalent sections are more harmoniously wedded elsewhere (in iv. 5, let us say) that is irrelevant, for equally a painter may blend his colours and textures on one canvas, and set them in crude contrast on another.

On this basis it may be possible to suggest the contrasting modes of thought-expression in Horace's lyric corpus, and show such contrasts actually at work within single odes; for that does occur, and in almost half the odes some sort of combined structure reveals itself.[1] Moreover, some special features of construction will call for comment; they have to do with continuity of sense or even, on occasions, with its studied disruption.

1. *The modes separately employed*

a. *Where there is no responsion*

This, one supposes, is the natural scheme for a lyric poet

---

[1] A brief sketch of the apparent thought-design of each of the odes (other than the purely informal, which are listed in the next two footnotes) is added below as an appendix to this chapter, except where an ode is treated at length in the intervening pages.

of the 'personal' tradition. Either he presents a single idea—possibly at some length, possibly with slight variations, possibly turned to display its facets—with no sense of antithesis or whole-and-part relationship; or else a sequence of ideas, strung together with more or less overt coherence, profits by an ingenuous absence of stylistic organization. In the former kind, the thought is static: all sixteen verses of i. 8 (*Lydia, dic per omnis*) are devoted to the single complaint against Lydia's corruption of a promising young athlete; twice a reminiscence of his former prowess intrudes (4, 11 f.), but there is no correspondence of parts or progress of ideas. The starting-point of i. 11 (*Tu ne quaesieris*) is Leuconoe's simpleminded enthusiasm for astrology; but Horace does no more than say 'carpe diem' in a series of aphorisms piled up in an almost Gilbertian manner. i. 20 (*Vile potabis modicis Sabinum*), as it stands in the received text, is a simple invitation-card in the polite and deprecating poetic vein; and the reproaches to Ligurinus (iv. 10, *O crudelis adhuc*) crystallize at the point where this unsatisfactory person is pictured gazing into his middle-aged mirror and lamenting his youthful waywardness—or his lost complexion. Twenty-three odes are of this simple type.[1] All are essentially expansions of a single thought, and the rarity of the type in the second and fourth books is noteworthy.

One notion above all must be left ringing in the ears of Sallustius Crispus, that it is wrong to be a hoarder of wealth, and his admonition begins and ends with it (ii. 2, *Nullus argento color est avaris*)—a suggestion of pattern we have perhaps seen in Sappho (and cf. i. 16). But the poem passes through various reflections on the control of the acquisitive urge which impart a sense of movement absent from the comparisons and *exempla* of i. 16, and the 'ring-structure' is less impressive than in

---

[1] i. 6, 8, 11, 16, 20, 23, 24, 26, 30, 34 (but perhaps progressive; see B. L. Ullman, *CJ*, 1936, 411 f.); ii. 20; iii. 10, 12, 15, 17, 20, 22 ,23, 25, 26; iv. 8 (but thought by Heinze to be responsive for the first twelve verses), 10, 13. (Fraenkel, 422, sees contrasting tone, of playful and solemn, between the first and second parts of iv. 8, the shift occurring after *v*. 12. But *v*. 30 at least, as Kiessling saw, subtly refers to the Stesichorean, Epicharmian, and Aristophanic Heracles.)

Sappho's poem: rather the ode is progressive. Under this heading it is convenient to set the thought of six odes,[1] of which iii. 30 is an intriguing specimen.

Horace's celebrated claim *non omnis moriar*, often referred to as an unnecessarily qualified one—cf. Fraenkel's remark (303 f.) on his 'enormous understatement'—deserves structural comment. It is only by stressing the particular symbolic picture of Rome drawn in the ode (another version of 'arce et urbe salva', like iii. 5. 11 f.), and by ignoring the city's 'eternity', that one can with any correctness say that Horace has in fact outlived his own prophecy: the priest and the Vestal no longer climb the Capitol, to be sure. But Horace's boast of being remembered in Apulia is much more of an understatement, while his opening phrases contain an unbridled *over*statement—for time and weather are not yet defeated, and the pyramids (and many an ancient bronze) are still going strong. The ode is basically uncertain and diffident in tone, and in structure is really a threepart run-down (cf. ii. 4. 13–24, iii. 14. 21–24, and see pp. 86, 120):[2]

vv. 1–5   I shall outlast all forces of the world and time . . .

6–9   well—I shall last as long as Rome, in her present form . . .

10–14   well—at least I shall be permanently famous in Apulia[3]

---

[1] i. 10, 29, 31; ii. 2 (but with slight 'ring-structure'); iii. 19, 30 (although this could be viewed as having three static sections with a coda; see p. 83, n. 2).

[2] The most dramatic occurrence of this feature of 'run-down' is at Virg. *Aen.* ii. 45–48, where Laocoon, putting forward his objections to the Wooden Horse, hits the nail on the head at once (*aut hoc inclusi ligno occultantur Achivi*); then, doubting his own imagination, wonders if the horse is no more than a superior sort of siege-engine; and in the end, surer of his own fears than of the nature of the thing feared, frankly gives it up (*aut aliquis latet error*).

[3] This is diffidence, but there is a touch of bravado which makes the mention of Apulia seem a sort of climax (but not a real climax; the examples quoted by Fraenkel, 305, show that the country birthplace is usually prouder of the poet than he of it). The mixture recurs, with reference to the condition of human life, in iv. 12 (see pp. 74 ff.). After the bitter *versus et cetera ludicra pono* (*Epi.* i. 1. 12), it is not surprising to find the popular reasons (or what Horace thought were the popular reasons) for the failure of the Odes put into Lollius' mouth at iv. 9. 1–4—and these are that Horace is a provincial (*longe sonantem natus ad Aufidum*, 2) as well as that his work is newfangled (3) and mere lyric (4). But the pessimism,

as a poor local boy who was first to make a certain poetic experiment.

14–16 Final prayer to the Muse, returning to something like the opening bravado—*sume superbiam quaesitam meritis*.

Although their structure is more complicated and they are discussed later in another category, i. 37 (*Nunc est bibendum*) and iii. 5 (*Caelo tonantem credidimus Iovem*) are good examples, in part at least, of progressive design.

β. *Where there is responsion*

By way of a general comparison of this category with the last-mentioned, something can be learned from parallel examination of the second and tenth odes of Book II. These two poems are not dissimilar in the patterning of their imagery and in manner both owe a debt to the Hellenistic diatribe.[1] What is more, they are both members of that notable group of poems wherein Horace, for reasons of political expediency and indeed of common sense, raps the knuckles of those who as 'the profiteers of the wars became imperceptibly the profiteers of the peace',[2] and who by their private behaviour seemed likely to imperil the general settlement. Nevertheless, in thought-structure the two odes stand apart. Where the address to Sallustius shows progress but not responsion of thought (beyond the last stanza's oblique reference, in *ingentis acervos*, to the *argenti* and *lamnae* of the first), that to Murena involves comparatively careful patterning of its two themes (the golden mean in behaviour, the inevitable but transitory nature of

---

or at least sadness, in that book is confined to life and love (iv. 1, 7, 10, 12, 13); in politics (iv. 4, 5, 14, 15) and in professional lyricism, so to speak (iv. 3, 6), bravado has become assurance (iv. 2 is a special case; see Fraenkel, 423 and 432 ff.). Indeed his Apulian origin is proudly carried as a title—cf. iv. 6. 27— and his 'home' river, Aufidus, is used to particularize a simile in the lofty Augustan ode iv. 14. 25 ff., as it did in the earlier and merely colloquial satire *S* i. 1. 58.   [1] See Heinimann, l.c. 201 and n. 53.

[2] Syme, *A Roman Post-Mortem*, 16. Those in question in the Odes are L. Munatius Plancus in i. 7 (see J. P. Elder, *CP*, 1953, 1 ff.); perhaps C. Sallustius Crispus in ii. 2; Q. Dellius in ii. 3 (see pp. 138 f.); L. Licinius Murena (Aulus Terentius Varro) in ii. 10 (on the identification, see W. C. McDermott, *TAPA*, 1941, 255 ff.; R. Hanslik, *Rh. Mus.* 1953, 282 ff.).

bad times). Thus, in ii. 10, the first four verses present both
themes:

> Rectius vives, Licini, neque altum
> semper urgendo neque, dum procellas
> cautus horrescis, nimium premendo
>   litus iniquum.

Now for eight verses the first theme is deployed through a
sequence of images and applications, from civilized life and
from nature:

> auream quisquis mediocritatem
> diligit, tutus caret obsoleti
> sordibus tecti, caret invidenda
>   sobrius aula.
>
> saepius ventis agitatur ingens
> pinus et celsae graviore casu
> decidunt turres feriuntque summos
>   fulgura montis.

Although the emphasis has been on prominence and excess
(*ingens, celsae, summos*), after the mention of *procellas* winds and
lightning have played an instrumental role in the development of the first theme. Now the second idea receives its
extended treatment:

> sperat infestis, metuit secundis
> alteram sortem bene praeparatum
> pectus, informis hiemes reducit
>   Iuppiter, idem
>
> summovet. non, si male nunc, et olim
> sic erit: quondam cithara tacentem
> suscitat Musam neque semper arcum
>   tendit Apollo.

A note on the behaviour of the sensible man enters into this
section, as the nastier sort of weather penetrated the preceding.
The themes must then be combined in an apodosis of positive
advice, for Murena must learn to face hard days in the sure
hope of better, and curb his exuberance when they come.
Knowing his man, Horace drops all suggestion that excessive

caution is likely to undo him;[1] one bears in mind the subsequent history of this fretful figure.

> rebus angustis animosus atque
> fortis appare; sapienter idem
> contrahes vento nimium secundo
>   turgida vela.

In this concluding stanza, in its nautical imagery structurally balancing the first, *angustis* and *secundo*, *sapienter* and *nimium* restate the themes. The ode is based in fact on a symmetrical plan of ideas, and is one of several in that respect.

It seems worth while to distinguish four main types within the responsive mode of writing:

(i) *Strophic*

Fourteen[2] of the odes have all the appearance of a balance of content parallel to the metrical correspondences of the formal Greek style; i. 19 divides itself into two distrophic groups, each strophe and antistrophe occupying four verses:

Mater saeva Cupidinum Thebanaeque iubet me Semelae puer et lasciva Licentia finitis animum reddere amoribus.	} *str. a* {	The gods of passion gather to press the old campaigner …
urit me Glycerae nitor splendentis Pario marmore purius: urit grata protervitas et vultus nimium lubricus aspici.	} *ant. a* {	… the particular vehicle of their power is presented.
in me tota ruens Venus Cyprum deseruit, nec patitur Scythas et versis animosum equis Parthum dicere nec quae nihil attinent.	} *str. b* {	Venus moves to the full-scale attack …
hic vivum mihi caespitem, hic verbenas, pueri, ponite turaque bimi cum patera meri: mactata veniet lenior hostia.	} *ant. b* {	but the victim resorts to man's remedy in such cases.

---

[1] As in the opening of ii. 3, two extremes are mentioned, but only *insolens laetitia* is really in point. (After my study of ii. 10 had reached these structural conclusions, I discovered that the 1–2–2–1 arrangement of the stanzas had already been stated by Enk, *Mnemosyne*, 1936–7, 171.)

[2] i. 2, 12, 13, 19, 38; ii. 8, 16, 19; iii. 2, 13, 18, 21, 28; iv. 12 (the *Carmen Saeculare* is of this pattern; but see pp. 107 f.).

The first eight verses report a *situation*; and the mustering of forces on the divine level in the strophe is opposed by the somewhat dazzling description of the relevant human beauty in the antistrophe. Then somes the *action*: attack and mental disruption, countered by a tried and trusted defence; and again there is a shift from god to man. This is all tiresomely obvious, no doubt, and as straightforward as iii. 9. Still, Horace does not always leave it as simple as this, and the borderline between strophic and symmetrical design is none too distinct. ii. 16 (*Otium divos rogat*) is a case in point: its thought-plan is not difficult, but by splitting the antistrophic movements (but not the strophic) into internal antitheta, and by inserting a central section which stands apart from the general scheme (as quite often, see below, p. 101), Horace has driven critics to probe and analyse and regroup the stanzas of this ode *ad nauseam*.[1] The opening shows an eight-verse movement: further it is right to recognize how the fifth and (much maligned) sixth stanzas demand each other, and how the words which close the second and eighth stanzas look forward respectively to the remarks which follow them.[2] This latter general observation is reinforced if one glances first at the triple anaphora of ideas between *vv.* 7–8 and 9–12 (*gemmis* 7 / *gazae* 9; *purpura* 7 / *consularis lictor* 9 f.; *auro* 10 / *laqueata tecta* 11 f.) which is not unlike that which ties together the first two stanzas of ii. 6 (see Wickham *ad loc.*), and then at the welding of *vv.* 31–32 with 33–40 (*mihi forsan, tibi quod negarit, porriget hora. | te greges centum . . . circum mugiunt,* etc. . . . *mihi parva rura et spiritum Graiae tenuem Camenae Parca . . . dedit,* etc.).

Therefore the analysis which commends itself most will be based on eight-verse and sixteen-verse units: so *vv.* 1–8 quote

---

[1] Büchner (*Bursians Jb.*, Suppl. Bd. 267, 1939, 135 f.; now see also *Humanitas Romana* (1957), 176 ff.) will have three groups of three stanzas (for their modal relation, see *Humanitas Romana*, 187) with the sixth stanza removed, as it was by Prien, Lehrs, Kiessling, and Heinze; K. Latte (*Philologus*, 1935, 301) and K. Barwick (*Rh. Mus.* 1950, 219) prefer five groups of two stanzas. See the bibliographical note of Burck, Kiessling–Heinze, i[8] (1955), 613, and add V. Pöschl, *Hermes*, 1956, 74 ff.

[2] See Barwick, op. cit. 252 ff.

the universal cry for *otium*[1] which cannot be bought (*str. a*), on which cue 9–16 moralize, but by contrasting the impotence of kings and magistrates and rich men in that connexion with the power for tranquillity of the simple life (*ant. a*). Then comes the interlude, a stationary two-stanza section of very general reflexion (17–24), placed in a pivotal position exactly as is the seventh stanza of ii. 2 (and not unlike the slightly 'offset' equivalent, 13–20 in ii. 13). There succeeds a repetition of the earlier scheme: after eight verses on the need to accept the bitter-sweet gifts of fortune (25–32 = *str. b*), another antistrophe with its own internal articulation (33–40) exemplifies the aphorism *nihil est ab omni parte beatum* (cf. Euripides, *Suppl.* 270, fr. 662 N) by setting side by side—and the reader can congratulate which he will—Grosphus' opulence and Horace's rural and mental gifts (*ant. b*).[2]

There seems no reason to elevate the use of two-stanza blocks in the odes just mentioned into an inescapable rule of Horatian sense-structure.[3] We shall see that this particular length is not at all universal in his responsive sections. An immediate instance to the contrary may be useful: in iv. 12 (*Iam veris comites*) there are seven stanzas; nothing appears to be purposely extraneous to the general sense and therefore able to be subtracted in the search for a pattern. And yet there is a striking contrast of tone within the ode. For twelve verses Horace signs a harmless spring song with familiar elements— the changing face of nature, the suitable mythical allusion, the evocative suggestion of Arcadia. Then this lulling atmosphere gives way to an extraordinary passage (13–24) of back-slapping heartiness. The guest is called to the wine-jars, while the host indulges in personal dig (*iuvenum nobilium cliens*) and arch witti-

---

[1] See Fraenkel, 211 ff.

[2] Büchner points out that the fifth stanza's first question is answered by the opening of the seventh stanza. It would be truer to say that both *vv.* 17 ff. (*quid brevi fortes iaculamur aevo multa?* etc.) and *vv.* 25 ff. (*laetus in praesens animus* etc.) pick up, chiastically, the 'timor' and 'cupido' of *vv.* 15 f. The first link integrates the 'inset' section; the second ties the two large divisions of basic pattern together.

[3] One must therefore disagree with Barwick, op. cit. 249 ff.

cism (*nardo parvus onyx eliciet cadum*, etc.—that is, a mere drop or two of the parfumier's product will win a whole flagon of the vintner's; what could be fairer—until one thinks of the price?). *Vv.* 19–20 read like an advertisement in the approved manner —and then more bluffness: *non ego te meis immunem meditor tingere poculis*). This overpowering manner is kept up to the end of the sixth stanza, and these twelve verses formally answer the first movement, for on second reading certain undertones are appreciated. Spring's return has an unmistakable underlying despair to those who have thought for a moment about the progress of human life; and even more compelling than the overt expression of iv. 7—and perhaps than the method we shall see in i. 4—is here the hint conveyed by the sorrowing cry of the swallow, whose personal history knows all the misery and waste of human tragedy (*vv.* 5–8). Now the bluffness of 13–24 is seen to be an assumed, unnatural, over-drawn pose, revealing here and there the real pessimism beneath. That is why the flagon is described as

> spes donare novas largus amaraque
> curarum eluere efficax

with which we may compare i. 7. 17 ff. and iii. 12. 2. 'To all sensitive and intelligent human beings a moment comes when they become aware that life is a dangerous and painful adventure, that ugliness and cruelty lurk behind every corner, and that only by shutting a door upon that knowledge is it possible to proceed.'[1] Horace never was, any more than Virgil,[2]

[1] Iris Origo, *Leopardi: a Study in Solitude*, 82 f. We should beware of thinking that Horace could never be like Leopardi; there are points of contact. The tone of the poems of the years of disillusion have affinities with the Italian; cf. esp. *Epi.* ii. 2. 53 f. with 'stanco mio cor'; or the Cinara passages, despite the utterly different past experience, with the poem *A Silvia*. The Roman Odes, like so much of Leopardi's work, combine national aspirations with a mounting pessimism; but for Horace mankind's unhappy lot is the result of wilfulness (*quid intactum nefasti liquimus?*) rather than of our 'basso stato e frale'. Of course, Leopardi sometimes quotes Horace.

[2] For the discussion as to whether the addressee is the Virgil we all know, as Bentley thought, see the bibliography of Burck, Kiessling–Heinze, i[8]. 616, and add Fraenkel, 418 n. 1. There is a distinct Virgilian tone in the second and third stanzas in particular (cf., for a rough guide, *vv.* 9–12 with *Ecl.* ii. 35, vi. 4–5,

a superficial and insensitive observer of the human comedy; and the humour of this ode is not even the usual Horatian banter, but tragic, and meant to be recognized, by one at least, as tragic. So in the final epodic stanza he unites these human attitudes, honest and false, setting after the philistine irreverence

> verum pone moras et studium lucri

the sombre reality, commonplace but effective,

> nigrorumque memor, dum licet, ignium

—and it is one who is wide awake to the lesson of nature and the condition of humanity who cries at last

> misce stultitiam consiliis brevem:
> dulce est desipere in loco.[1]

x. 26, 31–36; *G* i. 17; and *nigrorum ignium* recalls *Aen.* xi. 185–7); and one notes above all the mention of Arcadia (see Bowra's comment). This has naturally turned some scholars' minds towards the author of the *Aeneid*, while the unconvinced point to the 'unsuitable' phrases *iuvenum nobilium cliens* and *studium lucri*.

No interpretation of this poem seems to me to have done it justice, since Wilamowitz called the tune of unkind criticism (*Sappho und Simonides*, 321), and what is said in the analysis above makes Virgil, of all Horace's known friends, the *most* likely recipient of this disturbing recognition of the *lacrimae rerum*—and that Horace should have an acquaintance yet more susceptible to the pity and pathos of man's efforts to ignore the inevitable, and apparently bearing the same name, is hard to accept. As to suitability, other odes in this book would have shocked Virgil far more, especially 14, one imagines; and the wording of iv. 12 only shocks those who create for themselves a hypersensitive Virgil and are nonplussed on meeting his own robustness of speech (as when he 'licks his verses into shape'—Suet. *vit. Verg.* 22). *Iuvenum nobilium cliens* is an exaggerating expression, as the more difficult *studium lucri* must be (and a bluff joke, too); but the emperor had been *iuvenis* when he befriended Virgil many years ago. Virgil's death may well have occurred after this ode was written (for not all the odes of Book IV were necessarily written after 19 B.C.; iv. 7. 15 shows that that poem dates from a time when the plot, and importance, of the *Aeneid* were familiar to the Maecenate circle, but that need be no later than 23 B.C. when Books I–III appeared—cf. i. 7. 30 with *Aen.* i. 198 f., ii. 18. 26 ff. with *Aen.* ii. *fin.*, or iii. 3. 58 ff. with *Aen.* xii. 828). Fraenkel (418, n. 1) is scathing on the notion that Virgil could be so addressed in a poem *published* after his death; but 'the Augustan poets . . . when they published a book did not trouble . . . to eliminate from it everything that had been appropriate at the time of writing but proved less appropriate at the moment of publication' (idem, 287). Now see Perret, *Horace*, 179 ff. for more reasons why Virgil should not be banished from this ode.

[1] 'Misce'—i.e. by use of wine. The sentiment of this couplet is inverted by Housman, 'But men at whiles are sober / and think by fits and starts, / and if

There is a psychological credibility about this poem; further-more there is a neat triadic plan of thought, grouping the verses 12–12–4, the stanzas 3–3–1.

(ii) *Patterned*

Sometimes the parts of odes fit one with another into a pat-tern which gives articulation to the whole: the poet's meaning is by no means surging forward without control or ostensible continuity (and perhaps losing something thereby—certainly the intoxicating Pindaric sense of headlong gallop). But the patterning differs from strophic form, whether it has a sepa-rate origin or is a mere extension of that design. Of the seven[1] odes which seem alike in this respect, iii. 1 (*Odi profanum vulgus et arceo*) and iv. 5 (*Divis orte bonis*) are quite complex. Of the former (iii. 1) the first stanza is obviously a detach-able element, whether it is to be regarded as a preface to the whole series of Roman Odes or not.[2] Equally clear is the adoption, at least from *v*. 9, of the two-stanza block as a unit of sense (for a thorough grammar-break occurs after all even stanzas, but not after odd stanzas except the first), and we might be content to see here a monostrophic succession of self-contained γνῶμαι, each occupying eight verses.[3] And yet after *v*. 16 there seems to be a break in the thought: so far Horace has said that fate controls (and, by implication, death awaits) all alike; now he concerns himself with the different experience in life itself of the rich and powerful man on the one hand and the poor rustic on the other. This double theme pervades the last four eight-verse blocks; what is more, this section betrays its own interior design. *Vv*. 17–24 make the simple comparison: the countryman enjoys his food and can sleep, unlike the great man in his agonized existence. When the poet faces the dilemma

they think they fasten / their hands upon their hearts' (*Last Poems*, x. 4 ff.)—but the total message is the same as Horace's. The metrical equivalence of *stul-titiam* and *consiliis* is noteworthy, as also is the strength of the epodic transition-word *verum*. [1] i. 1, 15, 21; iii. 1, 16; iv. 5, 7.

[2] Solmsen, *AJP*, 1947, 337 ff.; Barwick, op. cit. 259 ff.; Fraenkel, 262.

[3] As Solmsen does, op. cit. 350 f., attributing to this a certain 'rigidity' in the ode.

of choosing which to emulate (41–48) he is in no doubt; and the contrast is repeated (*valle Sabina—divitias operosiores*). These are the outer blocks; inside them are two more, each of which dilates on one of these alternative conditions of life. The poor man of modest desires has no troubles; the violence of nature cannot touch him, for he has no vulnerable possessions on land or sea, nor does he try to control nature (25–32). The million-aire does try in his febrile fashion; but his mind is sick and his vulnerability to torment not lessened by yacht or horse (33–40). Returning now to the earlier part of the ode, and sub-tracting the opening personal manifesto, we find one general truth (5–8, the omnipotence of Jupiter) succeeded by the development of another at twice the length (9–16, wealth and status and behaviour do not deflect death). The formula for this ode is something like $x//a/bb//cd/dd//cc/cd$, loose enough to conceal the ground-plan, strict enough to prevent a feeling of formlessness.

The plea for the emperor's return is very similar (iv. 5). The people's eagerness for sight of him after long absence (first theme) is paraded in the first stanza, and followed by a stanza on the tonic effect of his presence (second theme). Then the first theme is picked up and deployed through a compelling simile by which may be known the fixity of Rome's longing for her leader; this takes two stanzas (9–16). But the deployment of the second theme is not to be restricted to a like dimension, and is to have antithetical arrangements of its own (like the second part of iii. 1). Let us see how it moves (17–40). First the attractions of the settled régime, dependent on Caesar's safety, are reviewed; 'he counts on his fingers the blessings of Augus-tan rule, each in a single line. Everything is regular, orderly, peaceful, in the rhythm as in the land':[1]

> tutus bos etenim rura perambulat;   17
> nutrit rura Ceres almaque Faustitas;
> pacatum volitant per mare navitae;
>   culpari metuit Fides;

[1] Wilkinson, 144.

nullis polluitur casta domus stupris;
Mos et Lex maculosum edomuit Nefas;
laudantur simili prole puerperae;
Culpam Poena premit comes.

This is in the nature of a 'state of the union' message; to be complete it needs the addition of a wider reference, to the stability of foreign affairs and the universal reliance on Augustus' power to keep things so:

quis Parthum paveat, quis gelidum Scythen,   25
quis Germania quos horrida parturit
fetus, incolumi Caesare? quis ferae
    bellum curet Hiberiae?

Now for the antistrophe to all this, the vignette of an individual Italian's day in this new, not to say novel, condition of civil and foreign peace:

condit quisque diem collibus in suis   29
et vitem viduas ducit ad arbores;
hinc ad vina redit laetus et alteris
    te mensis adhibet deum;

te multa prece, te prosequitur mero
defuso pateris et Laribus tuum
miscet numen, uti Graecia Castoris
    et magni memor Herculis.

and this somewhat vinous section (cf. *vitem, vina, mero*) has in turn its addition of universal relevance and acclaim—'we all so say, early or late, drunk or dry':

'longas o utinam, dux bone, ferias   37
praestes Hesperiae!' dicimus integro
sicci mane die, dicimus uvidi,
    cum sol Oceano subest.

The scheme will then be *ab//aa//b1b1b2/b3b3b4*, and as the seventh and tenth stanzas widen the picture, so the stanzas of narrower view are linked internally (by *culpari* (20) and *Culpam* (24), by *deum* (32) and *Herculis* (36)). And in each of these odes a final reprise of an earlier feature prevents a diffuse structure from falling apart (cf. iii. 1. 1 and 46/48 for first person verbs: iv. 5. 5 and 37 for *dux bone*).

(iii) *Symmetrical*

What may well be regarded as the extreme development of responsive form meets the eye in eight odes[1] of which the sense so arranges itself that an analysis based on meaning produces a symmetrical formula. The scherzo addressed to Aristius Fuscus (i. 22, *Integer vitae scelerisque purus*) has an imperfect structure in this respect—but purposely so, that the unbalance of the extremities may add piquancy to an ode full of wit and mockery:[2] it is a second reference to integrity and purity that one expects at the close, but by then Horace has changed his idea of the best defence of the unarmed poet abroad. The plan we start with then is this: a general and solemn truth (1–4), followed by the universal setting of its application (from far west to far east) (5–8), followed in turn by a relevant personal experience, much to the point and very exciting (9–12). Then this movement, stanza by stanza, reverses itself: the wolf in the forest looms larger than ever in the poet's memory (13–16)

---

[1] i. 22, 32, 33; ii. 10; iii. 9 (perhaps only (di)strophic: but the tightness of the responsion sets it apart, as does the careful insertion of Chloe—a disturbing element—into each distrophic section, at *vv.* 9, 10, 19), 29; iv. 1, 15.

[2] There is a neat suspense-device ('scene-pause-action' is the Horatian formula) in *me silva lupus* . . . (and then, much later, when Fuscus is hanging on the outcome) *fugit inermem*: cf. ii. 7. 13 f. *me per hostis Mercurius . . . sustulit*, or iii. 4. 9–13. (Likewise the girl's hiding place (*angulo*) is held back to the end of the distich at i. 9. 21 f. and *risit* is the delayed and unexpected climax at i. 10. 9–12.) Simple jokes in Lalage's ode are *arida nutrix, Iubae . . . leonum* (a mere *suggestio facetiarum*, as is *Bibuli . . . amphoram* at iii. 28. 8—and one sympathizes with the note appended to Sir Edward Marsh's translation of that ode), *militaris Daunias* (Horace's birthplace, of course!); and, more complex, the punning conjunction of Fuscus and (the swart denizens of) the Hydaspes, which picks up the pleasantry of *S* i. 9. 72 f. *huncine solem tam nigrum surrexe mihi!*, where Fuscus (*male salsus*) is on the scene. This last had become long since a standing joke, and is so referred to in the slave's appellation *fuscus Hydaspes* at *S* ii. 8. 14 (see R. J. Getty, *CP*, 1952, 106; and further R. G. Nisbet, *CQ*, 1959, 74). Fraenkel, making no reference to the purely verbal witticisms, would see a deeper feeling in the poem (Horace elsewhere claims that the gods protect a poet) than those of us who follow Kiessling; but he sees and describes well the symmetrical structure of the ode (185 ff.), as against Howald's (l.c. 68—see p. 128) and Heinimann's (l.c. 193 f.) idea of two-stanza blocks.

before he returns to underline the worldwide validity of his specific against such alarms, taking us this time from north to south (17–22 with overrun)—and then the surprise (all the greater because of '*integer*': cf. ii. 4. 22, iii. 7. 22): it was Lalage's name on his lips—and not a depressingly priggish virtue—that saved him (23–24).[1]

There are, however, odes with a somewhat different sort of symmetry. In these the ideas are not exactly repeated in an *abccba* fashion, but the sections of thought are balanced in terms of their respective length. iv. 1 is typical of the group (which includes i. 33 and iii. 29). Eight initial verses of personal application repeat the complaint which begins i. 19— and indeed quote that ode:

> Intermissa, Venus, diu
> rursus bella moves? parce precor, precor.
> non sum qualis eram bonae
> sub regno Cinarae. desine, dulcium
> mater saeva Cupidinum,
> circa lustra decem flectere mollibus
> iam durum imperiis: abi
> quo blandae iuvenum te revocant preces.

Then two groups of twelve verses (9–20, 21–32); the first recommends to the goddess the abode and temperament of Paullus (Fabius Maximus), a fitter wearer of her colours; the second compares the music and mirth of Paullus' home with Horace's own loveless and solemn present existence. Yet this has been no more than a fruitless delaying action;[2] Venus is not to be so denied. Eight more personal verses, of somewhat surprising tenor, complete the ode; we hear of an anguish of the poet's unknown to us before:

> sed cur heu, Ligurine, cur
> manat rara meas lacrima per genas?
> cur facunda parum decoro
> inter verba cadit lingua silentio?

---

[1] For, of course, *quisquis amator erit, Scythicis licet ambulet oris, nemo adeo ut noceat barbarus esse volet* (Prop. iii. 16. 13 f.).

[2] Fraenkel, 410 ff., has a most acute and helpful discussion of this poem.

nocturnis ego somniis
iam captum teneo, iam volucrem sequor
te per gramina Martii
campi, te per aquas, dure, volubilis. (33–40)

So, once or twice, shorter outer sections (with interrelated meaning to be sure: cf. iii. 29. 14 and 56) flank a longer central block with its own organization.

(iv) *Interwoven*

i. 14 (*O navis, referent in mare te novi fluctus*) is a signal instance of the interweaving of themes, where the striving for contrast-patterns even rejects the use of blocks in favour of 'two thematic ideas intertwined, and these form almost the entire material of the poem: A, the perils to which the allegorical ship is exposed . . . B, the resources the ship has for withstanding them or inspiring confidence'.[1] A *fluctus* . . . B *remigio* . . . B *malus* . . . A *Africo* . . . B *antennaeque* . . . B *funibus* . . . B *carinae* . . . A *aequor* . . . B *lintea* . . . B *di* . . . B *Pontica pinus* . . . B *pictis puppibus* . . . A *ventis* . . . A *aequora* (and one might add to A *saucius, gemant*, to B *filia nobilis* etc.). On the other hand, iii. 24 (*Intactis opulentior*) operates with the same device of interposition[2] but does not eschew the compartmental system: three blocks (1–8, 33–44, 54–64) which treat of current Roman vices (luxury—epitomized, as often, by the seashore villas of the very rich; greed for mercantile gain; physical and moral flabbiness, passing to the young) are set between examples of a saner, fresher way of life and calls for reform—so *campestres melius Scythae . . . vivunt*, etc.(9–24), and *o quisquis volet impias caedis et rabiem tollere civicam*, etc. (25–32); and later *vel nos in Capitolium*, etc. (45–54). This structure gives life and punch to what might have been only a querulous *convicium saeculi*.

II. *The modes in combination*

Many odes have two different modes of thought-sequence developed in succession and for that reason cannot hide an

[1] Tracy, l.c. 209 f.   [2] Heinimann, l.c. 202.

apparent split into discordant parts. The search for unity in them usually ends in a denial that there is any split at all, or the excuse that Horace was not at his best when he wrote the ode in question, or the reader is blamed for excessive literal-mindedness or some such fault. But this will not do, at least for odes like iii. 11 or iii. 27; and the discrepancy of the sections can be a matter of history.[1] More probably, these odes are indeed composite creations, but this composition is an architectural feature of the poet's own purposeful devising, and is to be appreciated initially at the level of structural analysis. It may react upon the thought—we shall see that it does. But first the schemes in juxtaposition can be studied for their own sake, and Horace's preferences noted.

a. *Where non-responsive sections are combined*

Fourteen odes add static passages together as two do progressive,[2] a simple pattern but not without its rhetorical counterparts. For example that relation, in terms of length and emphasis, of three sections which we call a tricolon is employed in i. 3 (*Sic te diva potens Cypri*)—though here it is a structure of thought rather than of words. For eight verses the poem concerns itself in propemptic fashion with Virgil's voyage to Greece. This prompts an exclamation of pious (and purely literary) horror at the intrepidity of the first sailor, which takes twelve verses. Thirdly the poet devotes twenty verses more to the theme

> audax omnia perpeti
> gens humana ruit per vetitum nefas

—a dire passage, from the first head-shaking *nequiquam* to the final *fulmina*. Not that tricolonic arrangement is confined to static presentation of the ideas, for one progress follows another

---

[1] As Fraenkel says of iii. 14 (*JRS*, 1946, 190) 'the two parts have different pedigrees'. (See also the same critic's *Horace*, 288 ff.)

[2] On the one hand i. 3, 25, 28, 35; ii. 11, 13, 15, 18 (but see below, p. 115); iii. 7, 8; iv. 3, 6, 11, 14; on the other i. 36 and 37. (But if the three-part descent of iii. 30 and the tricolon of i. 3 seem to a reader to be structurally indistinguishable, that is no great matter.)

in the same kind of way in the poem whose heroine is Cleopatra (i. 37). This seems to be the only ode of its type,
moving first through a sequence of present relief and joy and
reminiscence of the frightening past (1–12, despite the sentence-
end at 4); thence to a complacent comparison of the cham-
pions ranged on either side (12–21)—for now one can be sure
that the queen[1] was flown with wine as much as with success,
and that Caesar was moving swiftly and inevitably to bring
her downfall (from 6–12 we have two phases of her state of
mind; after 21 another). Then at the junction phrase *fatale
monstrum*[2] (21) begins the third sweep of reflection, admitting
with sympathetic insight (*saevis* 30 and *superbo* 31 are *her*
epithets) the thoroughly Roman behaviour of the queen in
defeat and restoring her to moral greatness (21–32: on which
see Fraenkel, 160). The important break here is at *v.* 21; and
this allows an antithesis of meaning to emerge as a function of
the design. i. 36 shows a double progressive design, with two
sections of ten verses each (for *v.* 10 is a transition (see p. 135),
belonging in syntax to the second half, but not yet part, in
sense, of the bibulous celebrations; rather it reinforces the
opening words of the poem). The first section pictures the
arrival of Numida from Spain; the second the party which
necessarily follows;[3] and in each part there is action and a
sequence of events. Just so, to return to the static type, do the
two halves of ii. 15 (*Iam pauca aratro iugera regiae*) stand in
direct opposition; the break in *v.* 10 divides the new days and
ways from the old. Or again, of the forty verses of *Ille et nefasto
te posuit die* (ii. 13) the first twenty (though subdivided) are
clearly of this world; 1–12 deplore one man's murderous in-
tent and 13–20 all men's blindness to sources of disaster; and
the rest, of vastly different tone, almost awed wonderment, are

[1] Or perhaps Antony: the ships lost in *v.* 13 were, historically, his (contrast
v. 24); perhaps the drunkenness was, too.

[2] Note the shifts: *columbas aut leporem . . . monstrum*, and *monstrum*; *quae . . . .*

[3] Campbell deserves sympathetic hearing for his attempt to remove Damalis
from the hard-drinking group of *vv.* 13 f. (see his edn. of 1945). She is much
engaged in the final tableau, and can hardly undertake so taxing a duty as to
be the life and soul of the party in two places and two respects at once.

set among the great figures in hell. If this division in form is again functional, we may be tempted to go so far as to see in the first section a demonstration of the weakness of man's efforts to save himself on earth, aimed at throwing into relief the power and self-assurance of the ἀνὴρ μουσικός, at least, in the underworld.[1]

A succession of static and progressive elements is fairly common.[2] The lush, not to say overpowering, scene in Pyrrha's grotto (i. 5. 1–5) gives way to a review of the misfortune of her swains, present and past (*fidem mutatosque deos flebit . . ., miseri quibus intemptata nites . . ., me . . . uvida suspendisse . . . vestimenta,* etc.). An even more determined drive forward closes the warning to Dellius (ii. 3), as one might well expect; the movement begins with the uncompromising *cedes* (17), repeated almost at once: then all resistance to the progress is pushed aside, and before the ode ends we are all with Charon and halfway across the Styx.[3] This is prefaced by a section with no such movement: the first sixteen verses form one stationary block in which the ideas turn back upon themselves (1 *rebus in arduis* / 5 *maestus omni tempore . . .*; 2 *in bonis . . . laetitia* / 6 *te . . . per dies festos . . . bearis . . .*; 9 *pinus . . . populus; lympha* / 13 *vina . . . unguenta; flores . . . rosae . . .*; 4 *moriture* / 15 *sororum fila . . . atra*).

If one looks for a half-and-half division under this heading, it is to be found in that wicked little piece of banter *Ne sit ancillae tibi amor pudori* (ii. 4). Horace brings to bear all the power of myth and poetry to excuse, nay dignify, Xanthias' infatuation with a slave girl; out come the precedents of Achilles, Ajax, and Agamemnon, and a whole stanza sets the

---

[1] This is the (not entirely convincing) view of Klingner, *EPMHNEIA, Festschrift Otto Regenbogen,* 119 ff.

[2] Fourteen odes have it: i. 5, 7, 17, 18 (but see Chap. IV, p. 148, n. 2), 27; ii. 1, 3, 4, 5, 9; iii. 5, 14, 27; iv. 4. The reverse arrangement is in ii. 6. In iii. 4 a progress is punctuated by static passages of admonition (not, as it happens, of the two-stanza 'inset' type: see pp. 86 f.).

[3] The synaphea and elisions of *vv.* 27–28 allow no pause at the climax. There are other, sidelong, effects—the pathetic repetitions (*omnes . . . omnium: serius ocius*) and the whirring of the sherd in the urn (*versatur urna serius ocius . . .*) before it jumps out. But these do not interrupt the progress.

reader in the atmosphere of the fall of Troy. So for half the ode : but although the second part takes its cue from the heroic scene, Xanthias is subjected (as Postgate suggests—see Gow *ad loc.*) to a neat process of deflation—Phyllis is, no doubt, of rich and royal stock (as were the Trojan captives)—well, if not quite that, not of the criminal classes, or anyway not of shameful birth—well, at least, not without physical charms, for example . . . at which point the victim at last seems to remonstrate, and the poet protests his own (at his age) purely academic interest in the matter.

Only one ode appears to show the reverse arrangement. In ii. 6 (*Septimi, Gadis aditure mecum*) Septimius' *cacoethes vagandi* is countered by a rejection of the places he would like to drag Horace to, and by the poet's own choice. But the ode then becomes static : when Tarentum has been named, there Horace stays, rehearsing its attractions until apt mention of his own demise *in situ*. Still, there was nothing against a more complicated scheme—the punctuating of a progress of thought by short static passages. And if iii. 4 (*Descende caelo et dic age tibia*) is to mean anything in the admonitory setting of the Roman Odes,[1] a separate status must be given to *vv.* 37–42 and 65–68 from the rest of the poem. A train of remarkably ingenuous notions (*me . . . ludo fatigatumque somno fronde nova puerum palumbes texere . . . non sine dis animosus infans . . . utcumque mecum vos eritis, libens insanientem navita Bosphorum temptabo,* etc.) introduces the Muses into the contemporary scene as an influence for moderation :

> vos lene consilium et datis et dato
> gaudetis almae.

Then another progress, in which Horace (as always) confuses the battles of the Titans with those of the Giants, and in which at the end he includes certain other violent characters (69–80), has inset in it the aphoristic stanza which warns against insensate force :

[1] Now see D. A. Malcolm, *CR*, 1955, 244.

vis consili expers mole ruit sua:
vim temperatam di quoque provehunt
in maius; idem odere viris
omne nefas animo moventis.

It is not often that (despite the precedent of the Pindaric γνώμη) relatively simple insertions of this sort occur, although small-scale internal *responsions* are to be found on occasions, e.g. in i. 1, iii. 29 (see below, pp. 90 ff.).

β. *Where the combination includes both responsive and non-responsive sections*

This is a more exciting possibility. Here eight odes are relevant, and Horace prefers to set the responsive design at the opening of the poem; only two odes work the reverse way.[1] ii. 12 (*Nolis longa ferae bella Numantiae*) will serve as a demonstration of the more common order. This *recusatio* starts with a triad—'you won't ask *me*, a lyricist, for epics of earlier wars [1–4 str.] . . . or divine iliads [5–9 ant.]; 'you have yourself a better medium and a better theme, Maecenas [9–12 ep.].' And now Maecenas' displeasure (at having his bluff called) must be forestalled and his attention diverted: hence the long preoccupation (13–28) with Terentia's beauty and warmth of love, loosely organized with a *me–tu* (13–21) opposition but essentially of a piece, and culminating in the final tableau of competitive kissing. The plan, as much as the topic, helps Horace to take the sting from his refusal; at the charming conclusion one has quite forgotten what he *was* talking about before.

ii. 14 (*Eheu fugaces*) almost looks like a *cento* of Horatian commonplaces—the inexorable flight of time, the tearless nether gods, the universality of death, the uselessness of attempts to evade it. No particular pattern emerges for sixteen verses, apart from a shift at *v.* 9 from the second to the universalizing first person plural. The four stanzas simply say that death has no regard for (1) character, (2) offerings, (3) status, (4) evasive

---

[1] The responsion comes first in i. 4, 9; ii. 7, 12; iii. 11; iv. 9; second in ii. 14; iv. 2.

action. But the ode, having much in common with ii. 3, is an open letter to a Roman gentleman (an ideal one, perhaps) of means, who would be concerned more at what he must leave behind at death than at the sights before him—(that is why, to Dellius, Horace uses that frightening word *exsilium*). And so the poem closes with a triad: the horrid prospect before the dying man is balanced by the happiness he must resign (*visendus—linquenda*), and the themes of positive torment and negative leaving-behind are joined in the epodic *absumet heres Caecuba*, etc.[1]

γ. *Where responsive sections are combined*

The use in one ode of two independent responsion patterns is not really parallel to the juxtaposition of non-responsive sections; the latter allows a contrast between 'static' and 'progressive' elements, but one looks in vain for a dynamic opposition of, say 'strophic' and 'symmetrical' in the former. These subdivisions do not all belong to the same level of analysis, in fact. Still, there are three odes in which one cannot help seeing more than one balanced design—ii. 17, iii. 3, and iii. 6. The first is, ominously, shorter than the others, and the received text is anything but encouraging. As it stands, the interweaving of *me* and *te* (and *mihi* and *tuis* etc.) persists until, from *v.* 21 onwards, a symmetrical antithesis develops (*utrumque* nostrum *incredibili modo consentit astrum* . . . te *Iovis* . . . *tutela* . . . *eripuit*, etc. . . . . me *truncus illapsus cerebro sustulerat*, etc.; and finally

> reddere victimas
> aedemque votivam *memento*:
> *nos* humilem feriemus agnam.

But this is a complicated poem, and merits further discussion

---

[1] Still, a Roman gentleman of Stoic persuasion might be somewhat less phlegmatic at losing wife and home than when faced with the sight of Sisyphus —and positively discomposed at the graphic preview of sacrilege among his wines. If anyone is, therefore, inclined to see here a mere climax of horror (disregarding *visendus, linquenda*) he may be right; and the ode will then be a combination of static and progressive sections. Three-stanza triads are rare in the Odes.

(see pp. 123 f.). The more spacious development of iii. 3 (*Iustum et tenacem propositi virum*) is rather more rewarding. The first four stanzas are not unreasonably taken as strophic (*aa/bb*—the praise of justice and resolution/the most celebrated exemplars of these qualities). Yet Juno's speech is no less so (and the syntactic connexion of *vv.* 16–17 is structurally meaningless except as a smooth welding of parts): five stanzas (17–36) admit the cessation of the past nuisance that was Troy (and confirm, briefly, the present respectability of Romulus); five more (37–56) conversely look to the future and the *imperium sine fine* and moral rectitude (49 ff.) of his new foundation (and, briefly, the forgetting of its Trojan origin). Then a three-stanza *condicio* (57–68) puts with singular directness what has been, in strophe and antistrophe, little more than a passing comparison between the accepted and the rejected—Rome's sound future depends on the firm understanding that Troy is not to be rebuilt. Thus the framework of this exciting but diffuse manifesto becomes clear. Not that this is quite the end of the ode: the final 'spell-breaking' stanza repeats a feature already known from ii. 1 (37–40) as a variant of a Horatian structural mannerism, the 'coda', although the sentiment is commonplace enough.[1]

All the odes have, in the possibly over-neat and over-terse conspectus above, been provisionally assigned to this or that category of design. Provisionally indeed; for a high degree of impressionistic identification of themes (and of their accompanying moods) is necessarily involved, and there is always the possibility that designs based purely on *mood* may be discerned in odes where the *theme*-treatment seems not to be structured of itself at all. Besides, the many textual problems which remain —and how many emendations in this particular corpus have won universal acceptance?—sap the confidence of arguments based on ostensible meaning. And structural analysis of this

---

[1] On the 'coda', see pp. 101 f.

sort cannot recommend this rather than that reading, or this rather than that order of stanzas, without a *petitio principii*. Yet the rewards of categorizing are sufficiently obvious, and two general judgements can be made: first, that the extraction of the bold patterns so far described is not vitiated by the possibility that we are embarking on an infinite process of analysis, descending to self-destroying subtleties; and secondly, that, crude as the type-divisions are, they are exact enough to minimize the chances of drawing false analogies from ode to ode, a tendency which one has observed among defenders of general theses.

As to the first point, there is for the most part little advantage in seeking one design *within* another; iii. 4 looks to be a special case. Any train of thought is, when all is said and done, a sequence of static notions; to stress the continuity is simply one way of looking at the matter. It is equally easy to insist on the forward movement of certain verses of a poem which as a whole is stationary. Even if responsion is used, static or moving passages within the parts of the responsive plan are regularly visible which have no relevance to the plan itself at all. We might expect an extended alternation of formal and informal sections in the same ode; but we should need several much longer odes than Horace gives us to establish this as an architectural feature. Quite often one type of section follows another, but there does not seem to be even a triple combination. Horace's experiments in design, therefore, although manifold and usually underestimated, are not so intricate as to resemble mere mathematical *tours de force*. Still, because a firm responsive arrangement can be felt (even if only half-consciously) at a first reading, he does now and again adopt a small-scale responsion for part of a larger plan, itself similarly balanced. Four odes are worth investigating in this way. In i. 1 (*Maecenas atavis edite regibus*) *vv.* 7–10 form the second block of the outer pattern but have an internal antithesis of their own, of public political acclaim and private agricultural satisfaction. Again, *vv.* 11–18 are at once two blocks in the general scheme and strophe and antistrophe in a plan of their own, setting land against sea as a source of gain:

gaudentem patrios findere sar- culo	luctantem Icariis fluctibus Afri- cum
agros Attalicis condicionibus	mercator metuens otium et oppidi
numquam dimoveas ut trabe Cypria	laudat rura sui; mox reficit ratis
Myrtoum pavidus nauta secet mare.	quassas, indocilis pauperiem pati.

Gaudentem and *luctantem* balance each other only formally; *metuens, rura, ratis* answer *agros, trabe, pavidus*: yet there is a contrast, for the merchant does, at least momentarily, envy the other's lot.

Whatever the true analysis of i. 12 (*Quem virum aut heroa*), there is a symmetry about the last three stanzas (49–60):

> gentis humanae pater atque custos,
> orte Saturno, *tibi* cura magni
> *Caesaris* fatis data: *tu* secundo
>   *Caesare* regnes.

> *ille* seu Parthos Latio imminentis
> egerit iusto domitos triumpho,
> sive subiectos Orientis orae
>   Seras et Indos,

> *te* minor laetum reget aequus orbem;
> *tu* gravi curru quaties Olympum,
> *tu* parum castis inimica mittes
>   fulmina lucis.

The first of these divides the honours between Augustus and Jupiter:[1] the second and third elevate each in turn, allowing them to share the intervening verse *te minor*, etc. (57). And iv. 1.

---

[1] Although *tu secundo Caesare regnes* is odd. Taken with *v.* 18 it asks for a revolutionary change in the relation of Jupiter to the universe: now he *will* have a junior colleague, as never before, if Roman prayers are granted. Moreover, its ambiguity is almost blasphemous, for in the other sense of the adjective (cf. *Iunone secunda* Virg. *Aen.* iv. 45, *secundo Marte* ibid. x. 21 f.; *secundis dis* Livy vii. 26) one piously expects *ille secundo Iove regnet* (cf. *v.* 57).

21–32 have a sub-structure of this kind—*illic* . . . (21 ff.), *illic* . . . (25 ff.), *me* . . . (29 ff.). Most intriguing of all is the fatalistic *Tyrrhena regum progenies* (iii. 29). The ode as a whole is a balanced arrangement of blocks (of 4, 8, 4 stanzas). But the central element of the triptych (17–48) has a strophic movement of its own, and within that passage again occurs a momentary blurring of an internal boundary; for at *v.* 41 the enjambement suggests the overflowing of the swollen river of the preceding simile. This ode is in the nature of a Chinese box (see pp. 113 f.).

Secondly, that there are enough differences in design to discourage easy analogies between odes will be clear from the detailed study of any supposedly similar group. Nor is any one analysis to be relied upon implicitly; that view will be best which gives a feeling of justice done and of more having been explained or brought to light in the poetry—and then only until a better comes along. Besides, structural analysis, like other sorts, is always aesthetic rather than 'drastic'—that is, the degree of intention on the poet's part is ultimately irrelevant. To be sure, he does not construct a careful triad of sense without realizing what he is doing; but the resulting composition as such and its relation to the whole lyric work of the author remains the prime object of study. Any alignment of ode with ode might therefore be defended, but it must not be superficial. Some would bracket together i. 4, 7, 28 and iii. 24.[1] And yet the last of these is not dichotomic as the others are; and only the first and last are at all 'responsive'. Another critic, exemplifying *compositio bipartita*, rightly to be recognized in Horace's lyric style, groups together i. 4, 7, 28 as showing harsh continuity (*iunctura dura*), while equating, as having easier transitions, i. 17, iii. 11, 27.[2] Yet the two latter odes are quite different in continuity as well as general design (see below, pp. 120 ff.). It is true that each devotes much space to the experiences and remarks of a mythical heroine, and has an internal division so clear that the first part seems no more than

---

[1] Heinimann, l.c. 194; Pasquali, *Orazio Lirico*, 712 ff.
[2] Kumaniecki, *Eos*, 1947, 7 ff.

an ἀφορμή for the second: but this makes it all the more hazardous to explain the problematical i. 15 on their analogy, for that has no equivalent schism.[1] Analysis by sections of two stanzas at a time has had its adherents: on this basis ii. 16, iii. 1, and iv. 5 have been declared closely linked in design.[2] Well, it may be so; but this sort of movement is not the whole story in ii. 16 or iii. 1, and seems flatly contradicted by the responsions and verbal echoes of iv. 5. In other words no ode can be called as evidence for the structure of another (or for the meaning of another, in so far as that is a function of the structure)[3] until thorough investigation of its own design has established it as a precedent within Horace's repertoire of schemata. For in fact every ode is in the last analysis unique and one does well to note the extent of Horace's experimentation with form. There is admittedly a great gulf of time and style between the Cleopatra ode and, say, the *Carmen Saeculare*; but the running and the responsive styles are not the terminal points of a progress of increasing sophistication—the landmarks are rather the various essays in combined design, the simultaneous display of responsion and progression (ii. 17. 17–32), the inclusion of pattern within pattern (iii. 29) and the final relaxation of the close marriage of thought-plan and verse-division (iv. 14).

Structural investigation may go a bit further. The designs are not necessarily to be regarded as something mistakenly uncovered, to be speedily and decently re-interred without comment. Form, in the sense of physical shape and mass, being an essential ingredient in a work of art, even where the

---

[1] Fraenkel, *JRS*, 1946, 189; again, *Horace*, 188 ff. (esp. 190 ff., where, to save this theory, iii. 11 and 27 are now said to have received unimportant preludes, to harmonize them with the erotic odes). If an ἀφορμή lurks in i. 15, which has no visible 'prelude' or 'protatic' characters, it can only be the reader's own awareness of recent events and his readiness to see an equation—which allows 'allusion', at least, to creep in; and one must remember Plutarch, *Comp. Demet. Ant.* 3. Now see Wilkinson, *CR*, 1959, 35 f.

[2] By Barwick, op. cit. 249 ff.

[3] See pp. 94 ff. This has nothing to do with attempts to deduce the sense and phraseology of particular verses from the ode-structure, as a guide to textual emendation. Such attempts are hazardous and rarely to be commended, unless other evidence points the same way.

appeal is to the ear, there is considerable aesthetic satisfaction in Horace's planning of the thought. But more than that, his almost Euripidean liking for dichotomy prompts the reader to look further and inquire whether Horace does not, now and then, make the form something other than an independent framework; does he, in fact, use it as a vehicle or a reinforcement of articulate meaning?

Possibly this is not a fair question—it is a leading question, certainly. Possibly meaning lurks in form only for those who are determined to see it there.[1] And frankly the evidence suggests that Horace did not regularly indulge in this subtlety; structural examination had best stop at the purely formal level. The sequence in i. 3 (*Sic te diva potens Cypri*) of blocks of eight, twelve, and twenty verses is only an adaptation of the common sentential tricolon; the meaning shifts from personal concern to fanciful moralizing, but the design has merely artistic affinities. Horace means to puzzle and surprise us, by giving us the story only in instalments, in i. 28 (*Te maris et terrae numeroque carentis harenae*); but this is a literary pleasantry which, like the same sort of effect in the second Epode, is quite divorced from what is plainly said in the actual words of the poem. The whole idea of balanced design, even in the physical aspects of the dance, no doubt largely answers to the ancient predilection for thesis and antithesis; and one is ill advised to seek significance in a mere feature of expression, even in compound odes. The praise of moral tenacity—including that of Augustus—and the speech of Juno on Rome's destiny in iii. 3 (*Iustum et tenacem propositi virum*) are of unequal length and unequal tone, the one terse and didactic, the other verbose and passionate: but beyond the artistic contrast no semantic value

---

[1] There is no intention here to quarrel with those who equate a poem's 'meaning' with its whole formal and sentential impact. There remains, however, for ancient poetry, which is neither mystic nor symbolist, a recognizable overt sense attached to the words used. i. 1 'means' that poetry is the most rewarding pursuit; i. 2 'means' that Augustus is a potential saviour for Rome; and so on. There is no inescapable connexion of 'meaning' with 'thought-arrangement'.

attaches to their juxtaposition. The second half of iv. 9 (*Ne forte credas interitura*) is bound to worry anyone who remembers Lollius' military setback of 17 B.C. and later comments on his way of life: and yet one cannot really think that Horace is using the *form* to suggest invidious comparisons.

But some odes give pause to judgment, for form undoubtedly assists sense more than once. Dellius is admonished—and the phenomenon of man's fool's errand to the grave is reinforced by the relentlessly moving description of the descent to the exile of death (ii. 3. 25–28). To ease his friend and patron's depression, Horace underlines his assurance that their fates are intertwined by the cross-weaving of *me . . . tuis, mihi . . . te, te . . . meae*, etc. (ii. 17). And perhaps form goes beyond mere assistance: an examination of i. 4 (*Solvitur acris hiems*) will be useful as a corrective to the tendency to more superficial analysis of this and other odes.[1] It has possibly the clearest dichotomy of any ode, a fact which encourages at the outset the use of a separate formula of analysis for each section. The metre is distichal, and the two sections show an uneven twelve-eight relation like the sixteen-twelve relationship of ii. 3. There is indeed in each of these odes a strong audible passage from form to form and from mood to mood; the unexpected *cedes* of ii. 3. 17 has its parallel in the explosive *pallida mors . . .* etc. of i. 4. 13. In each ode the first or strophic section is comparatively relaxed and expansive, the second or linear section oppressive and intense. The contrasts and antitheses of words underline those of the ideas. It is worth noticing for the moment simply the difference in mood between the two parts; the verbal economy of the second answering the prolixity of the first, and the everyday solidity of the first dissipated into the ghostliness of the second.

But there is more to this ode. It gives a good example of

[1] The analysis of i. 4 which follows is repeated, with only orthographic changes, from my article in *CP*, 1955, 164–6, with the retention of the copyright (1955) by the University of Chicago. I am grateful to the Director of the University of Chicago Press, and to the Editor of *Classical Philology*, for permission to reprint the passage here.

what can be done by combining the two techniques of thought production. The combination need not be merely artistic, either in the sense of adding variety, or in the sense of assisting to bring out the complete meaning: it can even replace overt statement of the poet's central idea. The structure can *be* the meaning, and here the technical contrast between the sections is significant in that sense. It is helpful to see how the ode (iv. 7), which has been called a recasting of i. 4[1] and conveys practically the same message, makes direct reference to the fundamental contrast between seasonal progress and return and the progress of human life with no return. Not only is the non-stop seasonal round stated with parallel fluidity of utterance (*vv.* 9–12), but the contrast is sharply pointed by the aphorism:

> damna tamen celeres reparant caelestia lunae:
> nos ubi decidimus
> quo pater Aeneas, quo Tullus dives et Ancus,
> pulvis et umbra sumus.   (13–16)

The sense of verse 13 has been clearer since Professor D. A. Kidd[2] decisively rejected the explanations of Kiessling and Lambinus and their respective followers and added his support to Doering's view that *damna caelestia* must refer to the passing of stars from the (night) sky, or else *caelestia* will be either otiose or meaningless. None the less Kidd's reference to the two(?)-monthly interval between the heliacal setting (hence *decidimus*) and rising of constellations does not allow *lunae* to mean much more than 'passing time'. It is more satisfactory to understand *lunae* as equivalent to *menses* and the latter to stand in opposition to *annus* (*v.* 7), each word having its astronomical meaning, that is, the twelfths or signs of the zodiac as opposed to the complete zodiacal circle.[3] Horace is making the point that from day to day the loss from the visible zodiac at the

---

[1] Wilkinson, 40.   [2] *CR*, 1948, 13.

[3] For *menses* so used cf. Manil. ii. 202, for *annus* Virg. *G* i. 6. Comparable is the use of *dies* for 'longitude' at Lucan vii. 189. (See R. J. Getty, *Studies in honour of Gilbert Norwood*, 172, 181.) Awareness of this circular form is seen in the etymological essay on *annus* in Varro, *LL* vi. 8.

western horizon at sunrise is balanced by the emergence of a fresh and equal section at the eastern, and from moon to moon the loss of a twelfth part by the appearance of a new twelfth. This conception has the merit not only of showing celestial reparation in general (as opposed to human life, where loss remains loss), but also of using the circular zodiac, as Catullus had used the sun's course, as a convenient symbol of the unbroken repetitiveness of the universal order.

The central idea is therefore presented in an allusive manner and duplicated in that the celestial reference reinforces the terrestrial, the two being inextricably fused in the Roman poetic mind; but the presentation is still explicit. On the other hand, in i. 4 the contrast is made by the structure, and is implicit. The first twelve verses describe natural change in terms of a thoroughly careful cyclic scheme; the last eight state the conditions of human existence in a linear sequence of three logical steps with a baldness of expression and an uncompromising directness that penetrates even the final 'digression'.[1] The first section subdivides itself initially into three groups of four verses with a general background first of day, then of moonlit night or underground darkness punctuated by the gleams of the smithy fire, then of day again, and this provides the basic symmetrical form. But the centre tetrastich further subdivides, and the subdivisions (5–6, 7–8) find their place in the outer scheme by looking respectively backwards and forward. In the full 4–2–2–4 verse-structure the thought reviews in turn men (and beasts) at, or ready for, work (1–4), gods at play (5–6), gods at work (7–8), and men (only, see p. 121) at, or ready for, play, for *caput impedire* is a sure promise of a party.[2] The second section, on the other hand,

---

[1] The last couplet cannot refer, as some would have it, to the actual experiences of Sestius' own youth. Where is the point in startling a man into realization of what death will take from him by mentioning delights age has already removed?

[2] This impression of symmetry would not survive if it were shown that Horace is describing a chronological sequence of spring scenes month by month, but this latter suggestion has been decisively rejected by P. Defourny in 'Le Printemps dans l'ode à Sestius (i. 4)', *Ét. Class.* 1946, 174 ff., who makes it

stating rather than describing, demonstrates linear progress thus: death is impartial and universal: therefore our life is finite and comparatively short (and precludes happiness founded on any other calculation): therefore you will soon die and on the instant lose the delights of this world, themselves subject to change. The temporal progress underlines the logical, as does the shift of person (*pauperum . . . regumque . . . nos . . . te*), and the unceasing forward movement is continued even to the *nunc–mox* opposition of the last verse. The contrast of form implies the essential contrast of sense, and is used precisely as the overt statement of iv. 7. The ode presents the reader with a mental diagram of its structure—a circle and a line; that diagram is the meaning.[1]

Finally we must not shut our eyes to certain oddities of structure in these poems. Of course, many aspects of the deployment of the thought are determined and made clear by the ground-plan of the ode in which they find themselves. Break an ode into its sections of sense and it at once appears that here is a central cleavage, here a sonnet-like division, here a tri-colon of ideas. To talk of 'change of tone', 'moving at a tangent', 'crescendo and diminuendo', and so on, is to put in other words the various structural types mentioned above.[2] Still, there are exceptional passages, which seem to be conscious attempts to secure—and sometimes to disrupt—smooth continuity.

Distinct sections are frequently set simply side by side with no binding element; indeed, binding is more usual inside sections. i. 9. 12–13 and iii. 6. 16–17 have this simple junction.

clear that the 'dramatic date' is April alone. (But Defourny can hardly be correct in thinking that the storms of spring are referred to at *vv.* 7–8: all the other pictures are of an essentially untroubled scene.)

[1] This is not to say that the diagrammatic method is the more successful. As H. D. F. Kitto remarks in another, but similar, connexion, 'We are not awarding certificates but comparing methods.'

[2] But not so accurately. The shift παρὰ προσδοκίαν at the close of i. 22 is not the same as that of i. 4 or i. 28. And does the end of ii. 3 move *crescendo* or *diminuendo*?

Of course with asyndetic arrangements there arises readily a feeling of strong opposition[1] and this is explosively reinforced by the labials of i. 4. 13 (*pallida mors aequo pulsat pede pauperum tabernas*). Yet Horace often contrives a 'lead-in'; as when the *laudes Lucretilis* of i. 17 pass to a review of the delights of a pro-jected house-party *via* a self-congratulatory beatitude:

> di me tuentur, dis pietas mea[2]
> et musa cordi est. hic tibi copia
>   manabit ad plenum benigno
>   ruris honorum opulenta cornu, etc.

By a rare variation of the norm, the parts of iii. 3 entwine even syntactically (16–17) as do those of i. 36; even more, one is carried almost imperceptibly into the second section of i. 7 (*Laudabunt alii claram Rhodon*)—for *vv.* 15 ff. seem at first to continue the subject and tenor of the earlier lines, before merging with the admonitory observations that follow. Now this lead-in sometimes appears as an overlapping section, so to speak, which is with difficulty—and no particular gain—assigned to this or that major division of the ode. Such is the transition-piece at i. 3. 21–24:

> nequiquam deus abscidit
> prudens Oceano dissociabili
>   terras, si tamen impiae
>   non tangenda rates transiliunt vada.

The superhuman daring of the first mariner, which has occu-pied the second section (9–20), is an understandable preface to the pious shaking of the head at human audacity in 21–40. Yet this first *locus* of the latter passage ('if God had meant us to

---

[1] Cf. the observation of Campbell (*Horace*, 228) on iii. 6. 44–45: 'even more effective . . . than the often and rightly praised terseness of the last three lines which anathematize four generations, even more effective, in my opinion, than the last line with its pair of words fitted with such a terrible convincingness to the metre, is the *suddenness* with which the "rhetorical question" breaks in upon the description of better times that were.'

[2] Horace and the gods are twice related in this verse, and the remaining two words limelight his observance of them and their protection of him. As to its seriousness, opinion will no doubt remain divided (of recent Oxford critics, contrast Fraenkel, 206 f., with Leishman, *Translating Horace*, 92).

go abroad he would have joined the lands together') picks up all the references to seafaring which have preceded, and is as much their climax as it is the starting-point of the theme *gens humana ruit per vetitum nefas.* Other overlaps are frequent:

i. 28. 17–20   General reflections, belonging to what precedes as much as to what follows,[1] on the variety but universality of death.

iii. 11. 25–29   Either the end of a responsive arrangement of the prayer to Mercury and the lute, or the start of the episode of Hypermestra, or both.[2]

iii. 14. 13–16   Either a private declaration of relief, matching the previous public thanksgiving, at Augustus' return and the maintenance of his rule, or the first intimation of the personal part of the ode and the party that is to come.[3]

iii. 27. 17–24   After the frightening list of omens which might have put Galatea off her journey, Horace blows up a storm to add to the joke; yet these stanzas likewise set the scene on to which Europe at once floats.

—and on a smaller scale, short anaphoric observations occur at i. 2. 29–30 and iv. 9. 29–30.

It may be worth while, in passing, to draw attention to places where Horace seems to secure his continuity by supposing some (unexpressed) objection or remark from his addressee or another. One can easily imagine a pause at i. 27. 18, while the miserable butt of Horace's banter whispers an ominous name in his tormentor's ear, and sets off so alarming a reaction.[4] Xanthias makes some move of remonstrance in the

---

[1] Campbell reverses the order of the couplets; then the first section will be the present *vv.* 1–16, 19–20, the second 17–18, 21–36. This gives a neatness of thought-movement which need not be Horatian.

[2] But if *vv.* 17–20 are accepted as genuine, *vv.* 25–29 cannot be admitted to the responsive schema of the ode's first part. See p. 122.

[3] This is seen and well put by Fraenkel, 290.

[4] More dramatic than Callimachus in a like scene (*Epig.* 43), Horace yet loses much of the whimsical delicacy of the Greek. As Callimachus' lovelorn young friend sighs, so do the rose petals in his chaplet collapse to the floor! (After writing the paragraph above I see that Fraenkel (180 ff.) refers this type of dramatic continuity to a possible source in Catullus xlii. For an application of the principle to iv. 7, see p. 112.)

last stanza of ii. 4 (and has perhaps been putting in the odd word of commendation for the girl; cf. *sic fidelem*, etc.) ; and has Valgius pleaded heroic precedents between *vv.* 12 and 13 of ii. 9?

As to breaking the continuity, or failing to strip his art of all that is unnecessary to pure form, Horace has an (almost Euripidean) inclination to insert or add certain passages which are aphoristic in content and complete in themselves, but which are quite extraneous to the poem's strict design. Especially does this occur with a two-stanza sequence (that is, eight verses in the quatrain metres, four in the distichal). Thus:

ii. 13. 13–20   An excursus on the *improvisa vis leti*, having neither the comically exaggerated righteous indignation of what goes before, nor the wide-eyed wonder of the tour of hell (21–40).
ii. 16. 17–24   'The sorrows of our proud and angry dust'.
iv. 4. 29–36   The rival merits of heredity and education (cf. Euripides, *Hecuba* 529 ff.).[1]

These last two passages being not without a bearing on the general scheme of the odes which enclose them (indeed in iv. 4 the point about *doctrina* vim *promovet* insitam, etc. must be made, in addition to *vv.* 25–28 on the *Augusti paternus animus*, or the Augustan–Claudian commission is not fulfilled), but their subtraction would, formally speaking, make no difference. On the other hand, we have at iv. 7. 17–20 purely assorted *loci* of very limited relevance indeed. In rather the same way, although the tone is different, the announcement of Maecenas' birthday at iv. 11. 13–20—the occasion of the feast and really of the poem—stands out markedly from the subtle and winning conversation Horace is having with Phyllis: while the laudatory formula of iv. 2. 37–40, however sincere, is equally adventitious and extraneous to the design.

At the end of an ode such a passage forms a *coda*. This is a well-known device, and with it Horace pulls up short at the

---

[1] This debate is in Pindar, too, although *he* had made up his mind (cf. *Ol.* ii. 86 ff., ix. 100 ff.; *Nem.* iii. 40 ff.; and Norwood, *Pindar*, 224 f. (n. 28)).

close of ii. 1 and iii. 3 and rebukes his Muse for absent-mindedly seizing the *plectrum maius*. Such renunciations are in themselves familiar enough from Theocritus and Callimachus, Virgil and Propertius. On the other hand Horace creates a variant on the *coda* form by setting in this position the moralizing two-stanza block we have already recognized. The prayer of i. 35 (*O diva, gratum quae regis Antium*) closes with a sudden introspective realization of the crimes and follies of the age (33–40). Similarly, after praising the cultivation of *virtus* for most of iii. 2 (*Angustam amice pauperiem pati*), the poet (borrowing from Simonides) commends in the last two stanzas somewhat less rugged qualities—a careful tongue, due observance of the gods, and the understanding that crime does not (usually) pay. And we can make what we like of the relation of the ideal happy man of iv. 9. 45–52 either to the praises of Lollius, the sketch of whose exemplary character ends (not before time, perhaps) at *v.* 44, or to the ode's opening essay on the power of lyric poetry. 'Ceterum censeo . . .', says Horace, and launches himself on a series of loosely appended complaints or beatitudes; and no doubt he felt this to be as good a way as any of rounding off a poem.

APPENDIX TO CHAPTER III

The Structure of Thought in 'Responsive' and 'Combined' Odes

THE contrasts examined in this chapter should enlighten many odes and be suggestive towards a fuller appreciation of others. For the reader to test how far the odes other than those treated at length above fit or fight with these formulae, a brief note of the apparent thought-structure of each ode is appended here; but the twenty-nine non-responsive, non-combined odes (listed on p. 68, n. 1, p. 69 n. 1) need no further mention and are omitted. The remainder are analysed in order of types (the index will trace individual odes). Previous essays in analysis are quoted where relevant and helpful.

Perhaps Prien should be given credit for the first systematic work in this field ('Der symmetrische Bau der Oden des Horaz', *Rh. Mus.* 1858, 321–76), but like others (Martin, Lehrs, Peerlkamp) he works from a preconception of Horatian faultlessness and treats anomalies surgically. Perhaps understandably, this type of structural criticism became for many years unfashionable ('mirum in modum neglegitur', wrote Enk in 1936) and is even today pursued spasmodically and half-heartedly. Enk's own often acute yet excessively terse treatment of the odes of the second book (*Mnemosyne*, 1936–7, 164 ff.) is preoccupied with the notion of symmetry and asymmetry, and is for most part purely stanzaic in approach. Sporadic remarks of insight and interest appear in Kiessling–Heinze, i⁸ (1955), A. Y. Campbell's edn.² of *Odes and Epodes* (1953: if edn.¹ is quoted, '1945' is added), and E. Fraenkel, *Horace* (1957). More important are the general treatments, *in parvo* that of H. L. Tracy in *Studies in honour of Gilbert Norwood* (1952), 203 ff.; *in multo* G. Daniels, *Die Strophengruppen in den Horazoden*, diss. Königsberg, 1940. G. Reincke, *De tripartita carminum Horatianorum structura*, diss. Berlin, 1929, has seemed more Procrustean and less fruitful.

Notes on 'interpretation' in the usual sense are added only where this is inextricable from the 'architecture'.

1. *Responsive*

(i) *Strophic*

i. 2   Thirteen four-verse stanzas arranged thus:
1–24 Strophe (3 stanzas) and equivalent antistrophe.
    25–28 Single pivotal stanza.
29–52 Further strophe and antistrophe.
In detail:
1–12 *str. a.* The problem: the weather brings fear of a new cataclysm—
13–24 *ant. a.*—or at least of civil strife.
    25–28 The question: *quem vocat divum populus?* (see Fraenkel, 247 n. 1).
29–40 *str. b.* A review of potential divine saviours—
41–52 *ant. b.*—and especial appeal to Mercury–Caesar.
See Tracy, 209. (The isolation of stanza 7 possibly commends the description 'patterned' for this ode; but the two groups of six stanzas before and after it are clearly strophic, and it is best listed here.)

i. 12   Block-structure of some sort has long been recognized. W.
Christ (*Metrik der Griechen und Römer*,[2] 654) argues for a
sequence of five 'triads'—based on Pindar, *Ol.* ii, and fully
formal—by stanzas marked *str.*, *ant.*, *ep.* Campbell's criticism of this, 180 f., is founded on a failure to appreciate the
Horatian and Pindaric peculiarities of method as set out
above, pp. 56 ff.; nor is he right (any more than Helm,
rev. of Daniels, *Phil. Woch.* 1942, 634 ff.) in seeing a major,
Greek–Roman division at *v.* 33: he prefers a grouping of
the stanzas as 3, 3; 2, 2; 1, 1; 3 (as against Helm's 3, 3, 2,
4, 3; Daniels agrees with Christ—3, 3, 3, 3, 3). Christ's
analysis must be divorced from over-strict adherence to
Pindar and divested of its meaningless *internal* division of
the thought of each of the three-stanza (i.e. 12-verse)
groups, which are to be recognized in our terms as single
'strophes', not triads, of sense—or else differentiated from
mere metrical units as '*quasi*-triads', as by Fraenkel, 292;
then Christ successfully demonstrates the ode's (monostrophic) movement:

1–12 *str. a.* The question: *quem sumis celebrare, Clio?* . . .
      virum . . . heroa . . . deum? The art then typified by
      Orpheus.

13–24 *str. b.* First answer: the gods.

25–36 *str. c.* Second answer: the heroes (from Hercules,
      Castor, and Pollux to Roman kings).

37–48 *str. d.* Third answer: Roman historical figures, lead-
      ing to the Julian house and its connexions, especially
      with the house of Marcellus.

49–60 *str. e.* Final answer: with reflex to first. Augustus,
      Jupiter's earthly vice-gerent, and Jupiter himself above
      all.

See now Fraenkel, 292. The supposed Greek–Roman split
at *vv.* 32/3 is not really defensible, as the deities and semi-
deities are in any case Roman by 'incorporation', so to
speak, as is the name *Liber* (cf. *Virgo*): the only inescapably
Greek section—the second stanza—owes its form to its
subject (the poet's literary 'ancestor'—Orpheus). One must
admit that *vv.* 33–40 read easily together, but the received
text at 35 f. (odd as it is to find Cato of Utica in that company) at least provides a full stop without which *memorem*

and *referam* struggle for mastery in an ill-organized sentence (as with Hamacher's *catenis nobilitatum Regulum*, etc.). Bentley's *anne Curti* saves the syntax but leaves the heroic assortment odd. Perhaps we must accept Cato for the present as a modern equivalent of distant semi-divine, semi-historical figures (cf. ii. 1. 24). But even if the candidates for inclusion after Romulus are not *persons* (so Fraenkel, 295 and n. 2: but cf. *fama Marcelli, Iulium sidus* in the 'men'-section: likewise, in i. 3, *Herculeus labor* alongside *Iapeti genus* and *Daedalus*), they are still mortal activities, and some sort of transition occurs hereabouts. To be honest, on the face of it the ode runs in stanza-groups thus: 3, 3, 2; 3, 1, 3 (note the quite different phraseology of the isolated stanza 12—similes are admitted for the only time in the poem, a Bacchylidean, or even Sapphic, touch to a Pindaric creation). This is like no other 'responsive' ode and cannot really be called a pattern. Yet one can hardly assign this ode to the non-responsive list, any more than i. 22 is to be expelled from the 'symmetrical' odes because of its twisted ending. The first and the last three-stanza groups are well-knit, and the Pindaric connexion unmistakable.

i. 13 Five strophes, each of four verses (that is, a 'block' in this type of metre (see Postgate, *CR*, 1918, 23 ff.) :

1–4 *str. a.* Horace's pangs of jealousy . . .

5–8 *str. b.* . . . his Sapphic symptoms . . .

9–12 *str. c.* . . . and fury at the visible marks of his rival on Lydia's person.

13–16 *str. d.* A sour forecast of the transitory nature of the rival's violent affection . . .

17–20 *str. e.* . . . and a praising of constancy.

In that the last eight verses are a counterblast to the twelve preceding, the ode shows a 'sonnet-like' division (cf. i. 4, ii. 3).

i. 19 See pp. 72 f.

i. 38 Strophe and antistrophe, each of a single stanza:

1–4 *str.* Horace rejects ostentatious luxury . . .

5–8 *ant.* . . . and demands simplicity as he drinks his wine. *Persicos* opens the strophe, and is answered by *simplici* in the antistrophe: *philyra* and *rosa* are countered by *myrto* and *vite.*

ii. 8   Three strophes, each of eight verses, but two themes:
(a) perjury, and (b) the success of beauty:

1–8 $a+b$. $\left\{\begin{array}{l}\text{Barine is forsworn but unpunished …}\\ \text{ … and the magnet of the young men's}\\ \text{attention.}\end{array}\right.$

9–16 *a.* Her broken oaths are by her mother's ashes, the
   stars, the gods …
   … but the gods are merely amused at her behaviour.
17–24 *b.* New lovers and old surround her …
   … whose parents—or wives—live in anxiety.
Peierati (1) and *votis* (6) anticipate the second strophe;
iuvenum publica cura (7 f.) is answered by the third. Indeed,
in so far as the first eight verses combine the themes which
are stated separately thereafter, the structure is, as it were,
a *triad in reverse.*

ii. 16   See pp. 73 f.

ii. 19   See p. 127.

iii. 2   Strophe (3 stanzas); antistrophe (3 stanzas); coda (2
stanzas):
1–12 *str.* Plea for hardy living: the exemplary warrior and
   his impact on a beleaguered city and its defenders.
13–24 *ant.* γνῶμαι on patriotic death and *virtus.*
25–32 *coda*—an additional moralizing passage, loosely attached, on *fidele silentium* in particular.

iii. 13 Strophe and antistrophe, each of two stanzas:
1–8 *str.* Offer of sacrifice.
9–16 *ant. Laudatio.*
For the relation to other Horatian 'hymn' forms, see p. 127
(and cf. iii. 18): The last stanza is, of course, self-advertisement for the poet, and the ode may be said to have a 'plot'
(see E. M. W. Tillyard, *Poetry Direct and Oblique*, 206 ff.).

iii. 18 Like the above, in structure and in hymnic form; see p. 127.
1–8 *str.* Invocation and offer of sacrifice.
9–16 *ant.* Italian country festival, in Faunus' honour, described (by way of *laudatio*).

iii. 21 Again hymnic in form (Norden, *Agnostos Theos*, 143 ff.,
161 f.); see p. 127. Here the strophe and antistrophe have
three stanzas each:

1–12 *str.* Invocation (and reassurance of 'deity' as to Corvinus' 'piety').

13–24 *ant. Laudatio.*

iii. 28 Strophe and antistrophe, each of eight verses (i.e. two stanzas):

To ensure the success of his evening with Lyde, Horace . . .

1–8 *str.* . . . calls for the wine . . .

9–16 *ant.* . . . and makes out the musical programme.

The wine and the music keep strictly to their own sections of the ode. Wilkinson, 148 f., treats this poem delightfully; but his tricolonic structure is hard to defend here (except by laying excessive stress on the mere fullstop after *v.* 4), and the last verse is not a 'coda' in our sense.

iv. 12 See pp. 74 ff.

Carmen Saeculare

The structure of the *Carm. Saec.* was determined to a large extent by the nature and details of the ceremonies to which it was appended (e.g. sacrifices and prayers to one group of supernal, one of infernal deities; the choirs of 27 boys and 27 girls), and its analysis is therefore irrelevant to the corpus of Odes, where the types of construction are calculated artistic variations, even where embracing some previous tradition.

In passing it may be said that theories of antiphonal singing between the girls and the boys are unsatisfactory (e.g. Gow's suggestions, cdn., 358): only the ninth stanza shows any sort of split (and if i. 21. 1–2 and 5–12 suggest that each sex is the special *tutela* of Diana and Apollo respectively, one should correct this by thinking of iv. 6. 31–33 and Catullus xxxiv. 1). The affinities with i. 12 (and a 'Pindaric' scheme) are clear enough: now see the treatment by Fraenkel (his chapter vii) and his references to Mommsen, Vahlen, Menozzi, and Redslob. The last two analyse the ode into six three-stanza groups (misleadingly called 'triads'—see above on i. 12): and Fraenkel (371) further arranges these (following Mommsen in seeing a major break at *vv.* 36–37) in two separate movements, each of nine stanzas. (The last stanza (73–76) is clearly a coda or epilogue; the choir sing of themselves (first person singular), somewhat on the *poscit opem chorus et praesentia numina sentit* principle). But it remains odd that *v.* 37 should denote a strong transition only by inference from *v.* 49 (i.e. *bobus albis* alone explains that *vestrum* = 'Iovis et Iunonis').

(ii) *Patterned*

i. 1 Daniels groups the verses 10+8, 10+8; Helm (reviewing him, *Phil. Woch.* 1942, col. 635) prefers 2; 4, 4, 4, 4, 4; 6, 6; 2, and Tracy, 208 f., 2; 4, 4, 4, 4, 4; 3, 3, 3, 3; 2. Campbell, 1 ff., and with some variation Norberg (*Uppsala Universitets Årsskrift*, 1945, 6, 7 f.) see a special connexion between *vv.* 3–6 and 29–34 (cf. the combination of athlete, general, and poet in iv. 3): but see Carlsson, *Eranos*, 1946, 404 ff. The first and last couplets certainly look to be outside the general scheme; they might read continuously, were it not for the *quodsi*, which takes account of what intervenes. This is the apparent structure:

1–2 Maecenas' attention is called

3–6 *a*		Olympic Victory	⎫	
7–10 *b*	b_1 (2 *vv.*)	Public Office	⎬ ambitions	
	b_2 (2 *vv.*)	Private Wealth	of the	
11–18 *c*	c_1 (4 *vv.*)	Farming	⎬ energetic	
	c_2 (4 *vv.*)	Trade	⎭	
19–22 *x*		Country Idleness—delight of the indolent		

23–28 *d*	d_1 (fused in	Warfare ⎫ delight of some	
	d_2 6 *vv.*)	Hunting ⎭ enthusiasts	
29–34 *y*		Lyric Poetry—delight of Horace himself	

35–36 Maecenas' approbation will assist Horace towards *his* ambition.

(The above scheme would be set askew by the Pontanus–Housman punctuation—a strong stop after *v.* 5 instead of after *v.* 6: but see Campbell, 3.)

The first part reviews varied applications of energy to the securing of a goal: one strophe (*b*) has internal antithesis (*hunc . . . illum*), and two others (c_1, c_2) build a private antithetical design (see pp. 90 f.). All this is corrected by *x*, which shows peace, relaxation, and the goal attained by one human type, at least (i.e. a provisional resolution, for *est qui* . . . (19), answering *sunt quos* . . . (3) after the manner of *Epi.* ii. 2. 182, suggests Horace's own liking). The second part has signs of internal responsion, *y* correcting *d* as to the true field for enthusiasm, the truly melodious instruments (*tibias, barbiton*, not *lituus* and *tuba*), the true source of cool pleasure (*gelidum nemus*, not *sub Iove frigido*). But the outer reference is to the calculating ambition of the first part (now replaced by enthusiasm), and to the sheer inertia of *x* (now replaced by artistic accomplishment). Only the athlete is comparable to the poet in approaching the divine (cf. Pindar's αἴγλα διόσδοτος)—hence *vv.* 6 and 30 are similar. (But that is their only relation, and the phraseology of 3–6 is mocking—cf. *pulverem collegisse.*)

i. 15   The final stanza presents a larger canvas, so to speak; hence *matronis* and *Iliacas domos.* (Yet Peerlkamp and Edwards have attacked it.) Campbell, 20, speaks of 'ring-structure', in the sense that the overthrow of Troy is the point of *mala avi* in *v.* 5. At any rate the last stanza is separable from its immediate predecessors.

With the received text the design is:

1–8 *a* The scene is set; Nereus begins his prophecy:

9–32 *b*
- 9–20 *b₁* The coming warfare; Paris' ineffectual skulking; and his inevitable death.
- 21–32 *b₂* The coming warriors; Paris' panic and flight.

33–36 *c* The final crash of Troy.

Müller's transference of *vv.* 21–32 to precede *v.* 13 achieves a neater development of sense, thus:

b_1 = 9–12, 21–28 The coming warfare and catalogue of warriors.

b_2 = 29–32, 13–20 Paris' flight from the field to Venus' protection and the boudoirs of the palace; and his inevitable death.

But it is hazardous to base the text on what 'feels better' in sense-analysis unless all the intricate variations and essays in form produced by Horace are thoroughly taken into account. As a matter of critical importance, it should be seen that, as they stand, 9–20 and 21–32 (my b_1, b_2) are virtually alternative treatments of the same sequence of ideas, as if Horace were loath to choose between two drafts and discard the merits of either. This odd feature might seem unbelievable did it not recur in iii. 16 (21–32 and 33–44); see below.

i. 21   1–4 *a* Girls, praise Diana; boys, Apollo and Latona.

5–12 *b* $\begin{cases} \text{5–8 } b_1 \text{ Girls, praise Diana and her haunts.} \\ \text{9–12 } b_2 \text{ Boys, praise Apollo and his haunts, his} \\ \quad \text{quiver and lyre.} \end{cases}$

13–16 *c* ἀποπομπή: thus assuredly will Apollo deflect disaster on to the heads of lesser breeds.

This ode is not symmetrical, despite the arrangement of the central stanzas. The first and last stanzas are not 'sung in unison'; indeed, we are here listening not to a choir, but to a choir's instructions. (For the 'hymnic' structure, see p. 126.) The deities are unevenly introduced also: the first stanza has a tricolon, in that Diana is unadorned, Apollo has one epithet and Latona two verses of description; but thereafter Apollo takes to himself the entire second half of the poem, Diana being perforce content with a single stanza (the second), while Latona's part diminishes to the hint in *natalemque* (10). Duhamel's *haec* in *v.* 13 (so also Bentley) is not structurally necessitated.

iii. 1   See pp. 77 f. The most recent 'traditional' treatment of the ode's unity is by V. Pöschl, *Harvard Studies in Classical Philology*, 1958, 333 ff.

iii. 16   1–16 *a* $\begin{cases} \text{1–8 } a_1 \quad \text{Heavenly proofs} \\ \text{9–16 } a_2 \quad \text{—and earthly} \end{cases}$ $\Big\}$ of the power of gold

17–20 *b* Horace's own horror of wealth and ostentation.

21–44 $\begin{cases} c\ \text{21–32 } c_1 \text{ Moderate desires gain heaven's favour:} \\ \quad \text{Horace richer than actual wealth could make} \\ \quad \text{him: his possessions reviewed and found satis-} \\ \quad \text{factory.} \\ \text{33–44 } c_2 \text{ Horace's possessions recognized to be} \\ \quad \text{modest but satisfactory: he is richer than ac-} \\ \quad \text{tual wealth could make him: moderate desires} \\ \quad \text{alone are satisfied, for God gives sufficiency.} \end{cases}$

This looks patterned: yet the sections c_1 and c_2 are no more than a double treatment of one idea, or perhaps alternative drafts (cf. i. 15 above). The removal of either *vv.* 21–32 or 33–44 would leave a satisfactory *a/b* (general/personal) distrophic form, in two groups of four stanzas, the first being *vv.* 1–16, the second 17–32, *or* 17–20 plus 33–44; but the text is not to be touched for that reason.

iv. 5   See pp. 78 f.

iv. 7   Since Housman's inarticulate adulation of *Diffugere nives* (and his own striking translation) it has been customary to rescue this ode, but not iv. 12, from Wilamowitzian oblivion ('two trivial spring songs', *Sappho and Simonides*, 321). With some diffidence, I prefer to do the opposite. On iv. 12 see above, pp. 74 ff.; as to iv. 7, on the maladroit use of mythology, see p. 19; and consider such uninspired epithets as 'pomifer Autumnus', 'manus avidas heredis'. (On the other hand *caelestia* may be doing a fuller job than is usually admitted (see p. 96 and n. 2) while the purely ornamental *splendida* and the bold Grecism *amico* could be textual faults (see Campbell *ad loc.*).) The overall message is nothing like so subtly conveyed as by i. 4 (the 'difference in weight' of the two odes has no relation to their difference in effect): the *loci* which we knew before Horace, and have heard repeated by him *ad nauseam* (cf. ii. 3, ii. 11, ii. 13, ii. 14 etc.), are heaped up again (*vv.* 13–28). For a similar 'heaping' see the series of 'old saws' in i. 11. Yet some of the expression is undeniably excellent—the speed of *vv.* 9–12 (like iii. 6. 45–48), and the triple *non* of *v.* 23, inexorably removing all man's worldly assets.

We may therefore expect also an unevenness of sense-structure. Clearly 17–20 look extraneous: the *proximity* of death has nothing to do with the rest of the ode; and that bogy, the *heres*, enters oddly here, as does the distressingly worldly advice of 19–20—Fraenkel's comment, 421, that 'one does not believe that the poet's heart is in it' is a far milder stricture than it deserves; and finally the scene is the underworld consistently from *v.* 14 to the end, if 17–20 are mentally subtracted. No doubt we are here dealing with another adventitious two-stanza 'inset'. The scheme may then be:

1–8 a_1 Spring returns, but passing time shows man's mortality . . .

9–16 a_2 . . . for the seasons revolve endlessly and a man's life does not.

17–20 *x* You *cannot* know the nearness of death; you *can* by determined selfishness foil your heir.

21–28 a_3 No quality or possession or connexion recalls a man from death.

This may qualify rather as a monostrophic design, to be sure.

(If there is any special point in addressing the ode to the eloquent pleader, Torquatus (cf. *v.* 23 and *Epi.* i. 5. 8 f.), it could be that we are meant to hear a cross-examination of the poet by him as the ode proceeds—(cf. i. 27):

1–6 'Spring returns and the earth is renewed.'

Q. 'Cannot human life then be so renewed?'

7–12 'No. Time changes one season rapidly and inexorably into the next.'

Q. 'Cannot human life be equally changeable, yet equally endless?'

13–18 'No. Unlike the seasons and stars we die for ever and do not know how soon.'

(19–20 . . . 'hence enjoy yourself and cheat your heir!')

Q. 'Is there no escape or recall?'

21–28 'None, despite all your assets.'

But this is a desperate device, and the *tamen* of *v.* 13 probably rules it out.)

(iii) *Symmetrical*

i. 22   See pp. 80 f.

i. 32   1–4 a_1 Appeal to the lute.

5–12 $\left\{ \begin{array}{l} b_1 \\ b_2 \end{array} \right\}$ Citation of Alcaeus as the *maestro*, in the singing both of adventure (b_1) and love (b_2).

13–16 a_2 Invocation of the lute.

The hymnic beginning and end are well shown by Fraenkel, 170 f. Note the further chiasmus whereby the references to the 'god' (*barbite, o decus, o laborum lenimen*) are bracketed by references to the 'worshipper' (*poscimus, vocanti*—the first and last words).

i. 33   Again the verses divide 4–8–4 (cf. i. 32), with the reference
          correspondingly particular–general–particular;
          1–4 a_1 Albius is consoled, as the innocent victim of a triangu-
              lar love affair.
          5–12 *b* 'These things work like that—*sic visum Veneri*.'
          13–16 a_2 Horace, too, has been so involved—and as a guilty
              party!
          Vv. 7–9 show that the 'triangles' are really groups in an end-
          less chain (cf. the Moschus original, quoted by Pasquali,
          Orazio Lirico, 496, with four lovers named).
              Helmbold's equation (*AJP*, 1956, 291 f.) of Horace's
          spurned *melior Venus* (13) with the Glycera who spurns
          Albius (2) would give a striking 'ring-structure'! But *iunior*
          (3) is then difficult, unless Albius is not only not Tibullus,
          but someone even more middle-aged than Horace himself
          poses as being in these lyrics. But of course *iunior* may de-
          pend on Glycera's unsupported word!

ii. 10   See pp. 70 ff.

iii. 9   See pp. 58 f.

iii. 29   As with i. 32 and 33, shorter outer sections flank a long
          central block, which here appears to have a triadic struc-
          ture of its own:
          1–16 *a* Maecenas is invited to exchange the 'smoke,
              opulence, and noise' of the city, and its accompanying
              tension, for the simplicity of the country.
          17–48 *b*. 'Let come what may.'
              17–28 *str*. Nature counsels relaxation; but you are too
                  concerned with politics and future events.
              28–41 *ant*. God hides the future; and events move like
                  a river, now calm now turbid.
              (Note how the 'nature' imagery is set in the first two
              stanzas of the strophe, the last two of the antistrophe. For
              such a chiasmus see Aesch. *Agam.* 984–9, and pp. 61 f.)
              41–48 *ep*. It is best to rely on the past, and ignore the
                  future.
              (Note the river's overflow from the metrical confines of
              the antistrophe into the epode at *v.* 41. This is the struc-
              tural counterpart to the hypermeter at *v.* 35, and to the
              grammatical continuity at 36/37.)

49–64 *c* Horace's own preparedness and simplicity of life guard him from the dangers of fickle fortune.

See also p. 92.

iv. 1 See pp. 81 f., 91 f.

iv. 15 1–4 a_1 False choice of subject for song, corrected into . . .

4–28 *b.* . . . praise of the Augustan age:

$\left\{\begin{array}{l} \text{4–16 } b_1 \text{ The régime's restorative value, for agriculture,} \\ \quad \text{public prestige, and morals . . .} \\ \text{17–28 } b_2 \text{ . . . and the citizens' freedom from fear of war,} \\ \quad \text{and safe observation of holy days . . .} \end{array}\right.$

29–32 a_2 . . . give the poet his true subject.

To be sure, either Phoebus is disregarded or else the correction of subject lies merely in giving a 'Julian' slant to it: otherwise it is hard to distinguish the last stanza's *virtute functos duces* and *Troiam* from the first's *proelia* and *victas urbis*.

(iv) *Interwoven*

i. 14 See p. 82.

iii. 24 See p. 82. Fraenkel, 240, rightly regards the structure as 'somewhat clumsy': interweaving by blocks rather than phrases is bound to be so. It was not repeated.

2. *Combined*

a. *Of non-responsive modes*

  (i) *Static+Static*

i. 3 See p. 83.

i. 25 1–8 The present: Lydia's fading powers of attraction.

9–20 The future: her complete breakdown.

i. 28 See, in general, Wilkinson, 109 ff.; Heinimann, *Mus. Helv.* 1952, 200. Most now accept it as a dramatic monologue, with an intentional withholding of the speaker's identity until late in the poem, as in *Epo.* ii. There is, of course, an ironical contrast between the fatalism of the first section and the superstition of the second.

1–16 (or 20) Apostrophe to Archytas: 'death comes to all'.

17 (or 21)–36 Apostrophe to '*nauta*': 'grant me a (token) burial'.

On the 'overlap' (17–20), and order of verses, see p. 100.

i. 35 1–28 Attributes and power of Fortuna.

29–32 The prayer: *serves . . . Caesarem.*

33–40 A static, moralizing, two-stanza passage (see p. 102) including an ἀποπομπή.

ii. 11 1–12 'Time and youth are flying: *linque severa.*'
13–24 Preparations for a convivial gathering.

ii. 13 See pp. 84 f., 101. Enk's chiastic analysis into 3+2, 2+3 stanzas (*Mnemosyne*, 1936/7, 172) is no better than earlier attempts quoted by him. The last five stanzas simply do not so divide. Dillenburger's 5+5 arrangement was safer.

ii. 15 1–10 The opulence and degeneracy of the modern fashion in house building.
10–20 The plain and spartan style of the old god-fearing days.
Despite his stanzaic approach, Enk (*Mnemosyne*, 1936–7, 172) admits a ten-verse structure here. Solmsen (*AJP*, 1947, 347) sees a shift towards the political sphere in the second half (the public–private comparison giving an internal antithesis).

ii. 18 1–14 Horace's own modest possessions (physical and mental) and happiness.
15–40 The febrile, insensitive, and futile behaviour of the wealthy.
Yet one is tempted here to establish two equal, strophic, balanced, sections, contrasting the way Horace lives and the behaviour of his unnamed *bête noire*, 1–14 and 15–28: then 29–40 will be an epode (of different length as usual) which equates their fate at last (*aequa tellus pauperi recluditur regumque pueris*—if that be the reading, for the scansion is anomalous in *v.* 34) but gives the poorer man the final advantage. Rich and poor meet (in prefatory fashion) in the strophe (10 f.) and the antistrophe (24 ff.). This will then be another 'strophic' ode. (Add this ode to those derived from Greek lyric: its theme and metrical type recall Bacchylides fr. 21 Snell.)

iii. 7 1–5 A consolation to Asterie . . .
5–22 . . . and a detailed assurance of Gyges' constancy.
And then:
22–32 Some stern words to Asterie herself, παρὰ προσδοκίαν.

iii. 8 1–12 Horace prepares to celebrate the anniversary of his escape from the falling tree.

13–28 Maecenas may use the occasion to escape the tension of public affairs.

iv. 3   1–12 The Muse's chosen one has his triumphs, unlike, but equal to, those of athlete or general.

13–24 Horace has his poetic triumph: he must owe it to the Muse.

There is 'ring-structure' here: *quem tu nascentem videris* is picked up by *totum muneris hoc tui est* and *quod spiro et placeo . . . tuum est*. Moreover, the parts are smoothly joined by the choice of Tibur as the Muse's chosen one's home in *v.* 10, which prepares for Horace's personal manifesto in the second half; and they are neatly balanced by the insertion of *Aeolio carmine* at the close of the first part, *Romanae lyrae* near the end of the second.

iv. 6   (For relation to other Horatian 'hymn' forms, see p. 126.)

1–24 Invocation and *laudatio* of Apollo.

25–28 The prayer—for Horace the Apulian poet.

29–44 Polite remarks to the choir (urging them to watch the rhythm, amongst other things) but all tending to self-advertisement for the author of the *Carmen Saeculare*.

See Fraenkel, 400 ff.

Dauniae decus Camenae (27) looks forward to *mihi . . . mei . . . Horati*, and links the prayer to what follows: the divisions are here less important than the continuity.

iv. 11   1–12 Preparations for festivity, which Horace hopes to share with Phyllis.

13–20 The occasion, by the way, is Maecenas' birthday.

21–36 By flattery, and by denigrating his rival, Horace tries to win Phyllis.

In a structural sense, 13–20 are a mere interruption to be disregarded: but there is nothing in the first three stanzas to warn Phyllis of the all-out attack of the last four, and the poem gains from division into three phases. 13–20 are of course important in Horace's own friendly and loyal relations with 'Maecenas meus'.

iv. 14   Here there are clearly separable elements; but it remains a matter of choice whether one views this sort of series as a combination of static parts or a progress of thought. (In i. 31 the final prayer arises very naturally from the preceding considerations.) A laudatory address to Augustus (1–6) and a review of the extent of his power (41–52) open and close this ode. In between sits an illustration of his greatness drawn from recent events (10–32), itself immediately bracketed by shorter passages which unmistakably assign to him all the credit (7–9, 33–40). (In fact 33–52 are an ἀρεταλογία of the type regular in hymns.) There are formal features present, but not the balance of size of parts needed for true responsion: nor are even the divisions of theme clearly marked. This elasticity may indicate a late stage in the development of thought-designs (cf. iv. 15); whether this is for better or worse it is for the reader's taste to decide.

(ii) *Progressive+Progressive*

i. 36   See p. 84.

i. 37   See p. 84.

(iii) *Static+Progressive*

i. 5   See p. 85. (A greater complexity is possible. Storrs (*Ad Pyrrham*, 5) believes in a symmetrical division: ' "who is your present lover?"—four and a half lines; "what grisly surprises await him!"—seven lines; "I'm clear, thank God!"—four and a half lines.')

i. 7   1–14 Tibur is praised above well-known places in Greece (for the Priamel form, cf. i. 1).

15–32 Horace counsels the use of wine—and the hope of more congenial surroundings—as a source of relaxation: this is exemplified by the episode of Teucer.

J. P. Elder (*CP*, 1953, 1 ff.) argues for a division into three sections (A 1–14; B 15–21; C 21–32), and interprets in terms of two specifics against distress of mind—wine and place. Certainly *Tiburis* (21) looks back to 12 ff., and *molli mero* (19) forward to *uda Lyaeo tempora* (22 f.) and *vino* (31), so linking B with A and C. But Teucer recommends wine and *hope* of new surroundings to his followers; and the *seu .. . seu* of 19–21 must imply that even a return to Tibur will not, alone, ease Plancus' nervous tension, as if actual place were *not* so important, after all, to human happiness. Therefore, despite the gliding continuity of 14–15 (Elder; and see p. 99), there is on the one hand an extraordinary and fundamental schism in the poem after *v.* 14, but on the other hand a mere passing from admonition to παράδειγμα at *v.* 21—a section-break which, however sudden, is like that of iii. 11 and iii. 27, which also pass from a 'prelude' to a dramatic episode including a speech.

This means that the ode has a diptychal outer scheme: the first part, which is of unparalleled length outside monostichal metres (fourteen verses instead of a multiple of four), dwells on Horace's own love for Tibur by means of a preamble structure. The second part is a παραμύθιον, having affinities with ii. 10 or ii. 9. 1 ff. in its weather-imagery, with i. 9 or i. 11 or ii. 7 in its recommendation of 'the cup that clears today of past regrets and future fears', and with iii. 3 or iii. 5 or iii. 11 or iii. 27 in its inclusion of a mythical episode. But the single link between the two major sections is Tibur; and this is a tactless link, for how would Plancus, chafing at being absent and occupied in arms (as we are led by Horace to believe he is), bear to hear the detailed praises of 'his' Tibur? The junction is unlike that found inside any other ode, adversative or corroborative: and the manuscripts which start a new poem at *v.* 15 (if perhaps simply misled by the superscription of the proto-type) deserve sympathy, although not support. Accepting Porphyrion's assurance that the ode is one, we seem to catch Horace here setting among his Parade Odes one of his bolder experiments. That is, he is possibly using, within a single poem, a typical *inter*-ode connexion (see Chapter II), of the type wherein a loose topical likeness is offset by a strong modal contrast. Thus he contrasts the contentment of his own life (of which Tibur and his love for it is a sym-bol) with the heartache of Plancus (which even Tibur might not assuage).

Yet even so the puzzle remains, and this ode largely re-sists analysis: it cannot be pretended that these ruminations offer a whole and satisfactory answer.

i. 17   1–12 The contentment and safety of Horace's estate, which is under Faunus' gentle tutelage.

13–14 A 'lead-in' passage (see pp. 99 ff.) prefacing . . .

14–28 . . . a forecast of the delights, especially of music and wine, awaiting Tyndaris at that estate. All will be peaceful.

The form of the last section is a tricolon (cf. ii. 5. 17–24 for the relative length of the *cola*, here of 2½, 4, and 8 verses respectively), and each *colon* is introduced by *hic*. The rivets which tie the first section to the last are 2 f. *igneam aestatem* . . . 17 f. *Caniculae aestus*: 9 *Martialis lupos* . . . 23 f. *cum Marte confundet Thyoneus proelia*: 10 ff. *dulci fistula valles personuere* . . . 17 ff. *in reducta valle* . . . *fide Teia dices*, etc. (as A. G. Lee has kindly and acutely pointed out).

i. 18   1–6 The power for good of wine (and love).

7–16 The dangers of excess, leading to a Bacchanalian picture, with the 'Deadly Sins', personified, among the rout.

i. 27   1–8 Horace calls for order amidst the drinking.

9–24 Himself challenged, he deflects attention upon Megilla's brother, at whose expense the company is diverted.
Cf. Callimachus, *Epigr.* 43. For Horace's 'dramatic pauses' in this ode, see p. 100.

ii. 1   1–16 Pollio is congratulated on his boldness (and versatility) in attempting contemporary epic.

17–36 A tribute to the vividness of his epic style leads to reflections on the *deum ira in rem Romanam* and its effects. Horace is in fact parading his own powers. (*Vv.* 29–36 form of themselves a two-stanza σχετλιασμός.)

37–40 The spell is broken; the *plectrum maius* dropped (cf. iii. 3. 69 ff.).

ii. 3   See p. 85.

ii. 4   See pp. 85 f.

ii. 5   1–16 'Lalage will love you in time . . .'

17–24 '. . . and outshine your former loves, Pholoe, and Chloris, and Gyges.'
The second section, not unlike ii. 12. 13–28, is a progress designed to lead the reader's thoughts away from something refused at the outset. The form is tricolonic, with the usual increase of colon-length: Pholoe figures in a single verse, Chloris in three, and Gyges in five.

ii. 9 1–17 Valgius is urged to dry his tears for Mystes' loss; the analogies are natural and mythical, but the passage does not progress. (Cf. *semper* 1, *usque* 4, *mensis per omnis* 6, *semper* 9, *omnis annos* 14 f., *semper* 17).

17–24 A better subject for song will be the triumphs of Caesar, in which we can move from topic to topic and place to place.

iii. 5 1–4 A hint on foreign policy?

5–12 Lack of moral fibre among the veterans of Carrhae.

13–56 The episode and speech of Regulus.

The continuity is interesting: *Persis* (4) suggests Carrhae and the too-contented prisoners; the latter, by contrast, induce Regulus.

iii. 14 The difference in tone, and in *persona* (see Chapter III, p. 100, and n. 3), is considerable between the two parts:

1–16 The civic welcome, as if prescribed with an official's voice, to Augustus on his return from Spain (see Fraenkel, 181 and n. 3).

17–28 A progress of entirely personal reflections: a celebration is to be arranged—an invitation sent to Neaera—which may get no further than her door—but the days for truculence are past.

But 13–16 can be regarded as a transition-passage (see p. 100).

The last part contains an implied parallelism between Horace's own departed bellicosity (as in 42 B.C.) and the increasing peacefulness of the times (so Campbell, *Horace*, 208). It also shows a notable run-down (cf. ii. 4. 13–24; iii. 30. 1–14):

'Tell Neaera to hurry ... to do her hair; of course, you may not even get so far ... very well, give up the attempt!'

iii. 27 1–16 Omens deprecated, but none the less *mentioned*, which might have put Galatea off her journey.

17–24 The gathering storm (see p. 100).

25–76 The episode of Europe.

Cf. iii. 11. It is debatable whether Galatea is purely 'protatic' or occupies *suo iure* a section of the poem no less important than the rest, and artistically independent: some

would see an antithesis of mood—frivolous, then serious—
but I cannot take Europe as tragically as she takes herself.

iv. 4   1–28 A Pindaric period in full flood, plus a Pindaric
parenthesis (*vv.* 18–22. cf. *Nem.* v, first epode), on
Drusus' Alpine War.

29–36 Two-stanza aphoristic passage; but here making the
essential point that the *patrum virtus* and *vis insita* of the
Claudii is a great power for good only when controlled
by the *doctrina* and *recti cultus* of the Augustan household.

37–76 Disquisition on the past service of the Claudii, and
the speech of Hannibal after Metaurus.

The last stanza of the first section prefaces the maxims of
29–36. The opening of the last section refers to the end of
the first (by the anaphora *Nerones . . . Neronibus*), and to its
own close (*Claudiae manus*). This latter section puts unch   arac-
teristic words into Hannibal's mouth: the *encomium Romanorum* and the imagery (and the reminiscences of the *Aeneid*)
should not disturb us, but the naked, and prophetic, adulation of princes in the last stanza is even more preposterous
as part of the speech (as it must be, in the absence of any
sign to the contrary: cf. Fraenkel, 428 n. 1), and thus perhaps typical of the less watchful artistry of the fourth book
as a whole.

(iv) *Progressive+Static*

ii. 6   See p. 86.

(iv a) *Progressive punctuated by Static*

iii. 4   See pp. 86 f.

β. *Of non-responsive and responsive modes*

(i) *Responsive+non-responsive*

i. 4   See pp. 95 ff. For the role of the animals in *vv.* 11–12 see
CP, 1955, 167.

i. 9   See pp. 65 ff.

ii. 7   See pp. 128 ff. Certainly not a tripartite arrangement
(2+3+2 stanzas: Draheim, Staedler), nor 'indivisible'
(Enk).

ii. 12   See p. 87.

iii. 11   This ode has many affinities with iii. 27, but the combination of thought-designs is not the same in the two odes. In

this case, it is not clear whether the first section is strophic, but there is a strong impression that it is (equally divided between invocation and ἀρεταλογία: cf. iii. 13, iii. 18, and especially iii. 21). But this depends on the presence of the fifth stanza, which has occasioned much adverse comment (to the list of complainants in Campbell, 103, add Buttmann; Maas, *Textual Criticism*, 34 f., takes it as an established interpolation), although Campbell, 104, is sure that a stanza of some sort stood there, and many believe the phrasing to be Horatian. Structural considerations are again a poor prop for textual criticism: there are enough examples among Horace's 'hymnic' odes to support either a strophic, or a quite uneven, division between prayer and praise (see p. 126). Accepting the Cerberus stanza we have the scheme:

1–12 *str.* Prayer to Mercury and the lute (to deal with Lyde).

13–24 *ant.* Attributes and power of this combined deity.

25–52 Progress from Lyde to the episode and speech of Hypermestra, itself a progress.

But the junction is smoothed by the use of the Danaids as a device of continuity, as Klingner points out (*JRS*, 1958, 175): the lute soothes them in the underworld (23–24), and they are a convenient παράδειγμα for Lyde (25 ff.).

iv. 9   1–12 *str.* Lyric poetry lives, like epic; so do its subjects.

13–24 *ant.* The figures of the Trojan war were neither unique nor first in the field (cf. *sola, primusve, semel, solus, primus*).

25–28 *ep.* Only the survival of poetry ensures the survival of the memory of heroes.

29–30 'Lead-in' to. . . .

30–44 . . . a listing of Lollius' claims to immortality.

45–52 Two-stanza coda: conventional moralizing.

It may be that the ode was written, as well as published, after the débâcle of 17 B.C. (but before its subject's moral downfall), purposely to defend Lollius' moral victories if not his strategy: then the phrases *animus . . . reiecit . . . dona*

nocentium, . . . *per obstantis catervas explicuit sua victor arma* may
be more pointed than merely fulsome.

(ii) *Non-responsive+responsive*

ii. 14   See pp. 87 f.

iv. 2   Heinimann (l.c. 202) sees a double-peaked movement in
this complex ode: first the rise to the Pindaric swan on the
wing and the fall to the Matine bee; then the rise to the
triumphal procession and the fall to Horace's own small
sacrifice. This may well be the supervening effect (and
there is certainly a typical *recusatio* division into (*a*) the
poet's own inadequacy, (*b*) someone else's better claim and
greater efficiency). But the ground-plan appears to be:

> 1–32 Non-responsive section of comparative literary criti-
> cism, closing with the direct antithesis (cf. *vv.* 25–32)
> between Pindar and Horace.

> 33–60 Linked to the above by *Antoni* (26) . . . *concines* (33)
> comes a 'patterned' formula. The praise of Augustus
> (now inescapable, however sincere) is introduced 'ap-
> parently in passing' (Fraenkel, 438) and therefore *vv.*
> 37–40 should be subtracted from the scheme. Thus:

> > 33–36 and 41–44 (8 verses) *Iullus* is to hymn Augustus'
> > return, and its attendant celebration, *maiore plectro.*

> > 45–52 (8 verses) *Horace*, with the crowd, will contribute
> > cheers (in homely rhythm), ritual cries, and incense.

> > 53–60 (8 verses) *Each* will offer sacrifice: Iullus twenty
> > head of cattle, Horace a single calf—which is worth
> > describing.

Note the sudden cursive movement at the close.

γ. *Of Responsive Modes*

ii. 17   See p. 88. The interweaving of the lives and experiences
of Horace and Maecenas is the point of the sense, and sense-
arrangement, of the poem. Campbell's suggestion, 60 f., of
nos for *me* in *vv.* 13 and 17 characteristically makes the
extraction of a scheme for the thought much easier—interweaving of persons for three stanzas, then combination for
one; combination for six verses, then antithesis (twice).
But this is not safe: the interrelation of pronouns does not
stop Horace confusing matters by undoubtedly using *nos*
for *ego* in his own half of the final contrast, in *v.* 32; and any

subtle analysis based on the pronouns may be wrong. It is best to say that an interwoven design passes smoothly to a formal (double) contrast from *v.* 22 on.

On the other hand there is a trace of progressive arrangement within *vv.* 21–30. Horoscopating signs suggest planetary influence: the influence of Jupiter as a planet leads to his intervention as a god: one divine rescuer recalls another (Faunus), and he yet another (Mercury). By the time of the sacrifice, the astrology is forgotten. I see no sign of the *planet* Mercury in *vv.* 29 f., as does Boll (*Philologus*, 1910, 164 ff.), whose Greek parallels are adequately countered by Heinze: in that case we should have to suppose Faunus not merely as the agent of another god (cf. i. 17, 1 ff. and 13 f.; and Pan is Hermes' son, of course) but as the agent of a heavenly body. But even if this view commends itself, there is still the phenomenon of one design inside another (but it will now be a chiastic scheme of planet–deity–planet).

iii. 3   See p. 89.
iii. 6   1–16 *Strophic* opening: cf. iii. 3.

  1–8 *str.* Horace admonishes the contemporary neglect of the temples and sovereignty of gods . . .

  9–16 *ant.* . . . and exemplifies the danger by recent disasters or narrow escapes.

  17–48 A *symmetrical* comparison of present moral collapse with ancient sturdiness of body and mind:

  17–20 x_1 (4 verses)—modern guilt, starting from flouting the marriage-tie, corrupts the offspring.

  21–32 *a* (12 verses)—the progress in profligacy of the modern sophisticated wife (and husband).

  33–44 *b* (12 verses)—the rugged decency of the republican rustic youth (and mother).

  45–48 x_2 (4 verses)—the extent and speed of moral corrosion over the generations.

For the (limited) insertion of one responsive section *within* another, or of non-responsive section *within* responsive and vice versa, see above on i. 1, ii. 17, iii. 29.

The analyses in Chapter III and this appendix may seem to some to be less satisfactory than those offered by other critics: and in some cases an alternative analysis has been suggested, or the one set out has been somewhat qualified. None the less, the following provisional figures will serve to show the proportion of types of thought-structure within the corpus as a whole, and within its two separate publications:

I. *The four books together*

	Simple odes	Combined odes	Total
Non-responsive odes	29	32	61
Responsive odes	31	3	34
Non-responsive and responsive odes .	..	8	8
	60	43	103

II. *Books I–III*

	Simple odes	Combined odes	Total
Non-responsive odes	26	27	53
Responsive odes	26	3	29
Non-responsive and responsive odes .	..	6	6
	52	36	88

III. *Book IV*

	Simple odes	Combined odes	Total
Non-responsive odes	3	5	8
Responsive odes	5	0	5
Non-responsive and responsive odes .	..	2	2
	8	7	15

(The *Carmen Saeculare* is simple, responsive.)

The two publications are notably alike, in that more than half the odes in each are simple in design, but at least half of these are responsive: again more than half of the total are non-responsive, but of these more than half are combined. In each case the proportion of simple odes to combined is identical (or practically so) with the proportion of non-responsive odes to those showing some responsion. A combination of responsive elements is rare in Books I–III, and does not appear in Book IV. This suggests that Horace did not materially alter his structural methods, in broad outline, as the years passed: nor does any sub-type significantly occur at, and only at, a calculable date of composition (the 'strophic' i. 2, i. 12, and iv. 12 are structurally much alike, as are iii. 1 and iv. 5;

conversely, the Roman Odes are very different each from each, only 3 and 6 seeming really similar).

Addendum: Hymnic odes in Horace

That Horace's development of these thought-patterns is highly original, and that he uses certain Greek contrasts merely as starting-points, is especially clear from his treatment of the hymn-form. This term covers, loosely, i. 10, 21, 30, 31, 32, 35; ii. 19; iii. 11, 13, 18, 21, 22, 25; iv. 6, 14; and *Carm. Saec.* The category cannot be too strictly defined, because i. 21 is primarily an address to a choir, although it shows three stanzas of praise and one of prayer; i. 32 is hymnic at start and finish (cf. Fraenkel, 170 f.); iii. 25 is a personal poetic manifesto in effect (one may call iii. 25 a 'dithyramb', but this does not help for comparative purposes). iv. 14 has hymnic elements sporadically within it, including an ἀρεταλογία—but of the emperor.

Now certainly ὕμνος was itself the label of a sufficiently elastic category, subdivided according to the god addressed—paean, dithyramb, etc.—or as to manner—euctic, cletic, apopemptic, etc.; but in its strictest form it was probably choric and monostrophic (so A. E. Harvey, *CQ*, 1955, 165 ff., who sees in ὁ κυρίως ὕμνος a religious poem sung to the lyre, with no physical convolutions by the singers). This hardly encourages the imposition by Horace of responsive thought to balance the loss of large-scale metrical pattern, for no 'triadic' or such complexities were traditional; but he varies his formula.

Sometimes the whole ode is stationary, or static sections succeed one another: i. 10 has static *laudatio* (but including a planned symmetry, perhaps; see Fraenkel, 162); i. 30 has a single thought (if a complicated tableau); i. 31 adds a prayer to a passage of introspection (the single θρῆνος, i. 24, is similarly static); iii. 22 is static and simple, although it can be analysed as invocation (one stanza) and dedication (one stanza); in i. 35 and iv. 6 the prayer, within a single stanza, comes after (respectively) seven and six stanzas of ἐπίκλησις and ἔπαινος, and is each time followed by a passage of personal reference (one plural and self-damnatory, the other singular and self-congratulatory—although oblique, being couched as encouragement to a choir). But see Fraenkel, 402 f.

But an appearance of responsive arrangement gives form to other hymns. The first part of iii. 11 (but see p. 122) sets twelve verses of invocation and request against twelve of praise and myth; iii. 21 does the same, except that the third stanza is comically digressive, as if reassuring the 'god' about a possibly unenthusiastic worshipper; ii. 19 divides itself into two groups of sixteen verses, with personal avowal of witness and belief in the former group (here including myth), praise and recitation of divine exploits in the latter. The second person pronoun is always to the fore in the laudatory strophe. The type established, some deviation creeps in: iii. 13 looks regular (1–8 offer of sacrifice, 9–16 *laudatio*, with *te . . . tu . . . tu . . . tuae* in the ἀρεταλογία sequence), but *vv.* 13 ff. are really a self-advertisement (see p. 106). iii. 18 has a first strophe of prayer and promise (1–8), but the second (9–16) pays the god the oblique compliment of depicting the happiness of the rustics at his annual festival (note *tibi . . . tibi*). (This freedom of form and of content is very clear in *Carm. Saec.*; *vv.* 49–60 are *laudes Augusti* (cf. iv. 5, 15), and the whole composition is really an *encomium Romanorum* (11 ff., 37 ff.). Now see Fraenkel, chapter vii.)

An Exercise in Comparison: the Ode to Pompeius

IF a moral emerges from the examination of the Odes which has occupied the previous chapters, it is that the critical reader will do well to take middle course between two extremes of appreciation. Let him avoid the rocks on the left hand, by refusing to regard each ode as a complete and purely inward-looking entity[1] and nothing more, without plunging into the hazard on the right, a whirlpool of cross-references and comparisons between the ode before him and many another. It is misleading—worse than that, it engulfs the immediate and generous response of the mind and the heart to poetry—if one pretends that without an intricate knowledge of matters which are not overtly expressed and of the phrasing, the thought, and the atmosphere of practically all the remaining poems of the corpus from which it is taken, the reader will be unable to find any meaning or any value in this or that ode, and this or that stanza.[2] To subscribe to this doctrine is to go beyond the

[1] But not avoid the rocks by so wide a berth as does, for instance, E. Howald, *Das Wesen der lateinischen Dichtung*, 64 ff., who rejects all notion of self-contained poems not only for Horace but for other Augustans and appeals to 'pure poetry' in a rather anarchic fashion (see Fraenkel, 208 and n. 3). One might see 'block' composition warring with ode boundaries at, for example; i. 17. 21–i. 19. 16 (see p. 49 of Chap. II), or i. 34. 14–i. 35. 32 or iv. 8–9. 30: but this is an exploitation of the potential connexion of poems in their arrangement in the collection as a whole (see Chap. II, where this feature is allowed for, *passim*), and not a composition-method. (After all, one might conversely point to 'interruption of blocks' at ii. 15, 16 . . . and 18, or i. 12 . . . and 14.)

[2] This is not to say that we should not learn, if we can, what literary associations are possessed by this or that idea or phrase in our poet, and study, say, the 'Bacchylides element in Horace'. In so far as, for a later writer, even the most prosaic and everyday object may only mentally exist inextricably wreathed about with strands of earlier poets' thoughts and locutions, to that extent the

realization that Horace's poetic locutions and constructions depend on combination and contrast; it is to transform the legitimate search for aesthetic and artistic form into a game of conundrums and secret passwords, where nothing makes any sense at all until matched with or complemented by something else. Besides, there may be lost all real chance of apprehending that very inner unity which lies at the heart of formal perfection.

But of course poets do not live in vacuums, or tie up their thoughts and words in so many separate bundles. Without doubt, each of these odes will reflect at various points on many another, and all will be enriched thereby. This is obvious enough in terms of verbal 'fields of association', or of the power of the poet's total utterance to enlarge the reader's sensibilities (if that is poetry's aim) : but beyond that there is an architectural factor, for analysis will have failed to do its job unless it establishes the patterns of internal structure, after it has laid them bare, as nothing more than different but closely related essays in form. Likely for other poets, this is overwhelmingly true for Horace's lyrics; and the collection must, at one level, be appraised as a structure of structures.

This takes us nearer to the whirlpool; it must not be allowed to swallow us. But it will do no harm if we succumb to the temptation to believe that Horace did not expect his public to assume an air of delighted surprise as at something wholly new as each ode was unrolled before its eyes (or ears). Far from each succeeding ode wiping away all memory of his earlier singing, it is impossible not to build up, as one reads or listens, a mental fabric of Horatian music and Horatian imagery, Horatian thought and Horatian expression (and of the Horatian system of relations between these items), and to set each freshly received utterance within this total context. This is very much as one member of a family takes from the most commonplace remark of another all the information revealed by overtones and covert associations and so learns of emotions and

critic who ignores the associations is cutting himself off from hope of full intellectual intercourse with his author.

wishes, physical and mental condition, attitudes to past quarrels or future plans, and much besides.[1] The result is a feast of impressions at various levels of apprehension, which must not become an orgy, blunting the senses. Provided only that the interpretation as such rests upon consideration of what is substantially like or surprisingly unlike the piece under review, then by means of controlled comparison understanding will be deeper and aesthetic satisfaction more complete.

An example is better than a deal of talk. Nothing will illuminate these last remarks, and at the same time draw together the threads of the earlier chapters, as well as a sustained comparative interpretation of even a single ode. The comparative net will need to be spread wider than it would be by the purely superficial reader, but severely restricted where erudition, worthier for its own sake than for increased understanding of a work of art, would luxuriate (for no two odes of Horace are entirely unalike, and there the danger lies). Let the specimen for this experiment be the seemingly not very remarkable ode ii. 7 (*O saepe mecum tempus in ultimum*), in which Horace welcomes home his friend Pompeius returning from the wars, and does so in somewhat excited locutions[2] but with a sequence

[1] This is by no means pugnaciously to assert Intentionalism or to set too little emphasis on the universal impact of a poem. It is simply a fact that any human utterance means more to a recipient who knows more.

[2] Excited and rather striking. This is so not only in the 'nova verba' *redonare, deproperare* (transitive), *parmula* (Niedermann's notion that *parma* is a back-formation from *parmula* (< *palmula* < *palma*, cf. παλ(ά)μη) is very doubtful. *Parma* is an Ennian word, *parmula* first in Horace), or in the 'party' words of foreign source, *ciboria, malobathrum*, or the curious *diem fregi* (cf. i. 1. 20 or iv. 5. 35 f. or *dum se calor frangat* Cic. *de Or.* i. 62. 265?); but in such subtleties as the *Doppelsinn* of *v.* 12 (do they bite the dust in death or in προσκύνησις?—the latter has the vote of Peerlkamp and others; see especially Kiessling–Heinze), and the startling *Quiritem* (cf. *o plebs* iii. 14) which conveys the soldier-civilian distinction so much more vividly since Caesar's famous brush with the mutinous tenth legion (Suet. *Iul.* 70)—not that the singular was Horace's invention (he uses it also at *Epi.* i. 6. 7), if the derivation is *co-ŭiriom > *Quirium, hence collective *Quirites* > *Quiris* (so Kretschmer, *Glotta* 10, 147 ff.; cf. the old funeral-cry *ollus quiris leto datus*, Festus, 254).

Notable too is the verbal anaphora—not merely the structural 'ties' which will be seen below—but also the picking up of the same word in a different sense after a brief interval (*celerem* 9 . . . *celer* 13; *fregi* 7 . . . *fracta* 11), a feature extremely common in Virgil (e.g. in *Aen.* iv, *fallere* 85, 96; *pendere* 79, 88; *exercere*

of thought which is all that could be expected ('How did *you* get home?'—'What times we had together!'—'Now let's celebrate!'). Seven pleasant stanzas, with many of the accepted Horatian ingredients—affectionate address to a friend; autobiographical tableau; reference to the beneficence of the gods, especially Mercury; notes on parties past and to come—one might feel confident enough to prophesy the course of the ode from start to finish. How then to gain greater insight into the poem as a piece of living, personal, and humane expression, as it purports to be? Of course, there are several ways of trying: but a succession of comparisons with other specially relevant odes in the collection will, as well as anything, add spirit and dimension to the verses on the page. Let four odes testify in order:

1. *The evidence of ii. 6*

The immediately preceding ode deserves to be taken into account first of all, simply because it stands where it does and establishes a prima facie likelihood of some sort of significant interrelationship, of topic or feeling or mood (see Chapter II), with the welcome to Pompeius. And the relation (of likeness and unlikeness) is indeed a close one—close enough to have encouraged in scholars such speculations as we have noticed[1] on the role supposedly played within *Odes* I–III by this pair, ii. 6 and 7. The verbal echoes give the cue: each addressee may be classified as a 'comrade in stress and danger', and so each ode places the keyword *mecum* (whatever its internal relations) at its beginning, and a form of *amicus* at its end; and the reference to fatigue and war-weariness in each has very similar expression (*sit modus lasso maris et viarum militiaeque* and *longaque fessum militia latus depone*). But in elaborating such individuality as each of these odes has, Horace employs a thorough opposition of elements of their content, a device with all the air of careful calculation, but whether at the time of composition

87, 100; *fovere* 193, 218; *reponere* 392, 403; *cogere* 406, 412–14—quite separate from 'normal' anaphora, as seen in *taciti . . . dissimulent* 289–91, *dissimulare . . . tacitus* 305 f.).   [1] See p. 44.

or merely of arrangement is another matter. The movement implied in ii. 6 is away from the city and home; the movement of ii. 7 is homeward, back to the old circle of acquaintance. In the discussion with Septimius all the energy is his, the lassitude on Horace's side: in the next ode, the characteristics are reversed. The *Weltschmerz*, or at least the air of adventurous past and valetudinarious present, is a mere scherzo in 6: in 7 Pompeius really is battered in body and so no doubt in mind too. The entire tone of the two conversations, so to call them,[1] is obtrusively contrasted. Septimius has all the vaguely directed but irresistible urge of youth[2] to be up and doing in the fields where history is being made or danger met for its own sake: and the reply?—'senectae', 'lasso', 'tepidas brumas', and all the signs of Horace's thinning blood and fading zeal, with as its climax the picture of the touching (and evidently not long to be delayed) funeral of the poet-recluse, attended by the dutiful tears of the friend who must clearly outlive him:

> ibi tu calentem
> debita sparges lacrima favillam
> vatis amici.

Naturally this is all part of the pose Horace is here pleased to assume. The attitude is of amused condescension of age to youth, of one whose iliads and odysseys are memories to one for whom they are still hopes, of (as Punch might have pictured it) Portly Uncle to Athletic Nephew who has suggested a Game of Leapfrog. Little touches assist this relationship: the response is larded with improving historical and geographical

---

[1] Not, however, in the sense in which i. 27 or possibly iv. 7 may be called 'conversations'. See p. 100.

[2] Septimius (who is made to speak to Horace as the poet in earlier days spoke to Maecenas—cf. *Epo.* i. 11 ff.) was young enough to need from Horace a letter of recommendation to assist his attempt to join Tiberius' *grex* some years later (*Epi.* i. 9). He was no doubt attracted by the constant military excursions of that prince, a fact which would seem to make the equation of 'gregis' in the *Epistle* with 'cohortis' practically inescapable, despite the reluctance of editors. For the general tone of this ode, cf. the similar witticism of Catullus xi, where the readiness of Furius and Aurelius for globe-trotting ensures that one may trust them to get as far as Lesbia's door.

footnotes on Tibur and Tarentum and the produce of the South Coast.

But Pompeius and Horace are of the same generation. The tone of their intercourse is in no way patronizing or mocking, but serious and sympathetic. There is room for humour in it, even a wild enjoyment; but the fun is shared, and there is stark reality under all that is said (*longa militia* means what it says, and the horrid suddenness of disaster is conveyed by the economical phrase *Philippos—et celerem fugam*). The longer one looks at the ode the clearer it becomes that there is strain and something forced in Horace's words of welcome, as if he is conscious (and in this how different from the ode before!) of not being quite master of the situation. Septimius gets as much twitting as he can take, perhaps more than he is likely to recognize for what it is: but to Pompeius the phraseology is kind and careful, as for instance in *cadis tibi destinatis,*—'we have been keeping these flagons especially for you!' There is much expression of friendly solidarity, so to speak,

—O saepe mecum tempus in ultimum deducte . . .
—. . . meorum prime sodalium . . .
—cum quo morantem saepe diem mero fregi . . .
—tecum Philippos et celerem fugam sensi . . .,

which is followed by the most politely oblique fashion of comparing experiences (and what these were, we shall shortly see)

sed me per hostis Mercurius celer
denso paventem sustulit aere;
te rursus in bellum resorbens
unda fretis tulit aestuosis.

Before any further explanations can be given or guessed at the thanksgiving—and the drinking—begins, and fatigue and painful memories start to fade. And the party is to be no merely lukewarm affair: the scale is lavish[1]—the wine Massic, the cups (probably large) to be filled to the brim (*exple*), the

[1] Cf. i. 9. 6 *large . . . benignius* (the latter is adverbial, of course, as Alcaeus' ἀφειδέως shows)—such open-handedness is a sign that the wine is a counter-attack against the forces of uncertainty and gloom.

perfumes poured from vast containers (*capacibus conchis*). One doubts if the symposiarch was likely to order much water to the wine. In effect the closing scene is somewhat overpowering, as unbelievable in its febrile, organized jollity as was the previous ode in its final preoccupation with quietude and death.

So much from one comparison; no doubt more would strike the eye after further glances. Already appreciation of the expression of the poet's own frame of mind, and of his friend's situation and character, has been enhanced: or at any rate the appetite for understanding has been whetted. But it remains possible that the appraisal has been too subjective: perhaps conventions are blinding the critic's eyes, and the remarks to Pompeius are no more than the polite noises automatically called forth from the human animal by the stimulus of the given situation: or, equally possibly, the poetic classification— the εἶδος[1]—carries them with it, and Horace (among others) will be found to say just the same elsewhere. Let another ode offer its contribution at this point:

2. *The evidence of i. 36*

Of course, a sub-class of lyrics having exclusively to do with returning warriors is a mirage (although Alcaeus' welcome of his brother, ἦλθες ἐκ περάτων γᾶς κτλ., fr. 50 D, Z 27 L–P, is relevant): but that does not prevent us from searching the Horatian lyric corpus for a comparable ode in which to study this poet's usage in this kind of social and poetical situation. The obvious place to look for the merely formulaic elements, to distinguish the recurrent features, irrelevant to personalities, from what is important and individual, will be (for a *privatus*) the ode which sees the safe return of Numida from warlike Spain, i. 36 (*Et ture et fidibus iuvat*). The affinities with the Pompeius-ode are clear enough: in both odes the returning comrade is, of course, named and we learn (roughly) where he has been; in both the gods are to get the sacrifice, and the

---

[1] See A. E. Harvey, *CQ*, 1955, 157 ff. *passim*.

credit, which is their due; in both there is happy reminiscence
of youthful days spent with bosom friends (*sodalis* being a keyword); and finally, in both poems the homecomer is promised
a party of the most animated kind, with all the appurtenances
of flowers, unguents, and wine in plenty. The very act of
enumerating these features, and so removing them in order to
concentrate on the significant variations, sets off in greater
clarity that which is individual and special. The Septimius-
ode cast light upon differences of mood and meaning in ii. 7:
but these were within the range of possibilities of divergence or
parallelism between contiguous odes (and part of the total
achievement we have already seen).[1] When Numida's welcome is carefully scanned, the differences between it and ii. 7
are suggestive less in an artistic than in a purely personal way.
Artistically, indeed, the likenesses predominate, and the structure of thought shared by these odes falls into the category of
'combined':[2] for each ode shows two major sections, the first
dwelling on the moment of joyous arrival, the second on the
necessary junketings which are to follow. So in iii. 14 (*Herculis
ritu*), *vv.* 1–16 (*Caesar repetit penatis*) thus divide themselves
from *vv.* 17–28 (*i pete unguentum . . . et coronas et cadum* etc.).
So it is in i. 36 (giving in effect an equal, ten-verse division—
see p. 84); so again in ii. 7, with a marked shift at verse 17
(*ergo . . .!*).

But personally the odes are mutually instructive rather when
they go their separate ways, and this they do notably. In
Numida's ode, it is he who takes the initiative. He comes in
like a gust of wind, offers the embraces, remembers Lamia and
their boyhood alliance—and does not bother to recall the recent war or to compare experiences (there is nothing beyond
Hesperia sospes ab ultima, in fact). His friends are ready to meet
him in a crowd, and on neither side is there a hint of weariness
or constraint. How different is it with Pompeius! The cries of

---

[1] In Chap. II.
[2] See above, pp. 84, 121. Latitude is still left for 'sub-types' (e.g. progres-
sive+progressive; responsive+non-responsive).

delighted recognition, of reminiscence, of sympathetic inquiry, are Horace's alone: if others are there we do not hear of them except indirectly (cf. the hint of *quem* . . . etc. in *v.* 25). The newcomer is to do nothing but sink wearily and gratefully into the shade and drink oblivion. All is pointed to him: with Numida the third person address throughout suffices, but with Pompeius it is *te, tecum*. For twenty verses he is made to share the limelight with Horace; and after the celebrations are set in train with orders to the slaves and (presumably) to other guests, Horace ends a final reference to himself with a return (oblique though it may be) to his friend (*recepto . . . amico*). The celebrations themselves, too, are widely separated in spirit between the poems. Nothing is needed among people so clearly extravert and hearty as Numida's circle to keep alive the gaiety—Damalis above all can see to that—and the host need do nothing but start things off and fade into the background, ready perhaps to restore order with an *impium lenite clamorem, sodales!* if need be. But he is in the centre of things to the end of ii. 7: placing Pompeius beneath the laurel, organizing the supplies, arranging for the dice to choose an *arbiter bibendi*, and generally giving a shining example of how all are expected to make this affair an unstinted success—*non ego sanius bacchabor Edonis*. These hints put us on the track of the personal relationships: if we doubted before, we know now that Horace is faced with a diffident fellow, tired of war but afraid of the friendly intercourse of peace,[1] aching for acceptance and the forgetting of past events and past mistakes; one in fact who needs the full attention of the welcomers and in whose case the celebrations must not be allowed to falter, or seem to falter, for a moment. Besides, the drinking at Numida's carouse is enjoyed for its own sake, has no ulterior motive, has indeed its own virtuosity (the *Threicia amystis* is evidently a notable test of prowess). In dealing with Pompeius the appeal is rather to Lyaeus, looser of cares,

oblivioso levia Massico ciboria exple . . .

[1] Let this be said now and argued later; see pp. 139 ff.

and there is something we might call 'harping' on the subject of wine

> —nec parce cadis tibi destinatis . . .
> —quem Venus arbitrum dicet bibendi? . . .
> —non ego sanius bacchabor Edonis . . .

—the wine, in fact, is of paramount importance and not to be forgotten for an instant, in amorous byplay or any other side issue. To spread our net momentarily wider, we may recall Horace's recipe for assuaging another friend's heartache:

> . . . sapiens finire memento
> tristitiam vitaeque labores
> molli, Plance, mero . . .
> . . . nunc vino pellite curas.
> (i. 7. 17 ff.; 31)

Why is all this? With so much now understood, of thought and expression, convention and novelty, we look for more. Is it possible to assist interpretation further by erecting a biography of Pompeius from fresh comparisons? And if so, where now to look?

3. *The evidence of ii. 3*

An inherent contrast-device in the Odes which will not have escaped the aware reader lies in the interplay of persons to whom odes are addressed. Some of these are real and Roman, others merely literary and Arcadian: and some are 'relevant', in the sense that the true inwardness of the poem is illuminated for us only when the character and biography of the addressee is fully known, while many are 'irrelevant', serving no worse and no better that would many another as the recipient of Horace's poetic confidences.[1] The comparative inquiry on ii. 7

---

[1] Scholiasts and critics tend to try to make all addressees 'relevant', a natural enough impulse; and a known, but irrelevant, addressee is rare, although the Censorinus of iv. 8 is such a one. Maecenas is a good example of how the ode, not the person, must be the criterion: he is 'irrelevant' in i. 1, ii. 20, and iii. 16 (or practically so, except as one of Horace's social assets; thus

has so far suggested that Pompeius is likely to prove a 'relevant' person. In order to fill out the details of this essay of interpretation, and to achieve in the end as complete as possible a statement of the poem's structure and texture and artistic 'meaning', it will be folly to disregard as inadmissible any evidence on subject-matter and personalities.

The search for an equivalent figure—one tossed about in the civil wars and receiving thereafter a 'pointed' poetic address from Horace—leads unerringly to the persona of ii. 3 (*Aequam memento rebus in arduis*), Q. Dellius.[1] That ode is frankly admonitory, even minatory: but its structure shows affinities with ii. 7, each being obviously diptychal, with very different sections and a strongly marked transition (in ii. 3 at *cedes . . .* 17). Now Horace's tone to Dellius indicates at once that character's toughness and exuberance—of his attitude to life the extreme of *laetitia* is really under attack, and so uncompromising an apostrophe as *moriture* leaves no doubt about the person so apostrophized. As it happens, we know quite enough of Dellius to confirm this first impression. If anyone profited from the 'wars of succession' it was he. Admittedly, no honest man could have pointed out a self-evident Right taking the field against an unmistakable Wrong: nor could the most clearsighted have forecast with certainty the attitudes of the protagonists to one another at any future date. Men like Ahenobarbus and even Messalla turned from this champion to that before being sure of supporting the side which (shall we say) did least violence to their own principles. But if Messalla himself could label Dellius above all 'the acrobat of the civil wars' it was because of a depressingly slick professionalism which characterized the zigzag career of this

these odes are merely 'dedicated' to him); but he is highly 'relevant' in ii. 12 and 17.

[1] The Blandini(an)us vetustissimus alone offers 'Gelli'. But Messalla's brother L. Gellius Publicola, untrustworthy as he may have been (Dio xlvii. 24), is scarcely so likely a recipient of this threatening and uncompromising admonition (on his eclipse, see Syme, *Roman Revolution*, 350); and no other Gellius suggests himself. The evidence of the remaining manuscripts, and of Porphyrion, in favour of Q. Dellius, is now generally accepted.

particular opportunist.¹ He left the side of Dolabella to join
Cassius in 43 B.C. not without expressing his readiness to
hasten his former chief's imminent downfall and death as an
earnest of his own new loyalty (if one may use that word here).
From Cassius he passed to Antony (and no evidence suggests
that he suffered on the losing side at Philippi—or was even
engaged in the second battle on Brutus' side). Then for a
decade he pursued the career of roving personal envoy for
Antony in the East, persuasive and complaisant, cynical and
shrewd, pleasing his master, it was said, with his body as with
his brain, adroitly avoiding the disaster with which Cleopatra's
envy might have overwhelmed him—and even chronicling the
Parthian War—until, just before Actium (and when his adherence to one side or the other was still a valuable commodity),
exempli sui tenax, as Velleius dryly puts it, he crossed to Augustus. Taking all he could from the war, he then flourished
materially in the peace: we need not doubt that *coemptis saltibus
et domo villaque flavus quam Tiberis lavit* refers directly to his
possessions. Before long he was officially recognized as *amicus*
of the emperor,² among the leading props of the régime which
now ensured his own prosperity. Little wonder if Horace feels
impelled to rap the knuckles of this shining example of adroit
materialism, venal attachment, and well-timed opportunism.

To all this Pompeius stands in striking antithesis. For certain, he was on the losing side at Philippi. It is hard to be sure
what precisely happened to him in and after the battle, but
Horace's words give some indirect information which is worth
thinking clearly about. Of himself, Horace says that he in-
gloriously tossed away his shield and fled, only (in his panic)
to be wrapped neatly in an obscuring cloud and lifted clear of
the field by the direct intervention of a god. Now, of course,
as we have often been reminded,³ here is a mixture of the real

<hr/>

¹ The sources are: Vell. Pat. ii. 84. 2; Dio xlix. 39. 2, l. 13. 8, 23. 1–3; Plut.
Ant. 25 and 59; Sen. *suas.* i. 7; Joseph. *Ant. Iud.* xv. 25–27.
² And indeed *primae admissionis*; see Sen. *de Clem.* i. 10. 1 (and J. A. Crook,
Consilium Principis, 23 and 162).
³ Wilkinson (60) puts it well: 'the shield that he admits with scarcely a blush

and the fanciful. Horace is using literary allusions, almost quotations, as conventional devices to refer obliquely to his own experience. The effect, even the intention, is to be as vague as possible about what really happened. Clearly in this ode Horace's aim is to welcome and to soothe his friend, equally clearly that friend performed no wonderful and courageous feat of arms which deserves to be mentioned, for the *virtus* is no more directly credited to him than inclusion among the *minaces*. Hence the tact which is universally agreed to be Horace's outstanding social characteristic[1] must be here in play, alike when he speaks of his own and his friend's *res gestae*. It is hard, therefore, to agree with a critic who, after acutely and rightly insisting on the need to ascertain Horace's own intention in this ode even after the literary borrowing has been seen for what it is, makes the confusion, of which these verses have occasioned much, even greater by a fresh interpretation of the drift of Horace's remarks hereabouts. Tactful and considerate of the other's feelings he certainly is: but not by insisting 'on such a drastic sign of cowardice' (i.e. *v.* 10) in himself or by speaking 'of his own soldierly deficiency in the crudest possible manner'.[2] To take his words so is to eat one's

(how this has worried some of his admirers!) to have left on the field of Philippi, had been left in a bush by Archilochus and before the walls of Sigeum by Alcaeus.' Admittedly Archilochus was being purposely shocking to the received code of his contemporaries, and Alcaeus may have indeed suffered the full indignity (cf. Hdt. v. 95). But for Horace there is no need to talk even of 'bravado' here (as does Mancuso, *Studi Funaioli*, 197 ff.). Fraenkel (11), on the strength of fr. 51 D, adds Anacreon to the list of rhipsaspids, and shows up (164 f.) the Homeric 'quotation' of *vv.* 13–14 for the literary joke it is (*Il.* xx. 443 f.; one may compare *sic me servavit Apollo* at *S* i. 9. 78, although it comes via Lucilius). For the order of words hereabouts, see Chap. I, p. 24, and Chap. III, p. 80, n. 2.

[1] Yet cf. the infelicities of *S* i. 5. 29 and ii. 1. 20; and *C* iii. 14. 1–4 after all say that Augustus has *not* succeeded in winning the *morte venalem laurum*, delightful as his victorious return may be, and *v.* 5 of that ode chooses an extraordinary attribute with which to honour Livia. The emperor perhaps defeated Horace's *sensus communis* until their friendship blossomed in Horace's later years. (Cf. i. 6. 5–8, where Horace claims not to be the type of poet to hymn Agrippa: 'for I cannot sing of sulky Achilles, untrustworthy Odysseus, or the internecine strife of Pelops' house'! One can of course define a gentleman as one who is never *un*consciously rude.)

[2] Fraenkel, 11 f. How much to take as factual in Horace's words is a problem.

cake and have it, for if Horace expected his readers to be cultivated enough not to take these words (and those concerning Mercury) seriously and realistically, then he cannot be using them to put a crude emphasis on his own shortcomings— the same phrases cannot be both literal and non-literal to the same people. Are we then to suppose that Pompeius will feel better because he alone will fail to grasp the allusions? But it is hardly to be supposed that an ignoramus capable of taking these words at their face value was Horace's boon companion in his Athens days, or even that two levels of understanding are to be assumed at all (as perhaps in ii. 6 or ii. 4).[1] Porphyrion's unimaginative misunderstanding of *vv.* 13–14 (for him the poet is *significans clam et quasi furto quodam se inde fugisse*) should not be disguised as crafty insight. Had Horace really escaped by running in utter panic or by skulking in a ditch or the like, he would have said so and served his purpose better by means of what Sellar calls 'his habitual candour and ironical self-depreciation'. But he did not so act and therefore cannot so speak.[2] In fact he carefully avoids attributing any

One could believe that, fighting in early winter over a marsh, he might find an opportune patch of mist (*denso aere*) for tactical use: and I should not like to venture an opinion on the degree of seriousness with which he assigns the credit for its appearance to Mercury, any more than I should on the seriousness of the respected citizens who have told me how Durham Cathedral was saved during the 'Baedeker' air-raids by the similar rising of a mist from the river on the most dangerous night, and have given the credit to St. Cuthbert.

[1] If Pompeius were literal-minded he would have objected if Horace had claimed to jettison a shield which as a tribune he did not possess: but the evidence on this point (tribune's personal arms) is curiously lacking, and this very passage is quoted as the decisive authority by P. Couissin, *Les Armes romaines*, 315, n. 2 (and 395, n. 3). All may turn, as R. P. Wright has remarked to me, on whether Horace had a horse or not: this is another thing we do not know. Simpler readers *might* take the description of events at its face value. Which raises the question: how serious *in their eyes* were Horace's references to the protective power of the Muses and Mercury and Faunus, especially the last named? (It is impossible to force a distinction between Horace's attitude to Mercury and to the others, or to the Muses and to the others. ii. 17. 28 ff. equate Faunus and Mercury; while iii. 4. 25–27 equate the Muses with the two gods by giving the Muses the credit for acts of salvation elsewhere attributed to Mercury (ii. 7. 13) and Faunus (ii. 17. 28).)

[2] Fraenkel very rightly insists (14, 260, 298) that Horace never tells downright lies about himself. (Edelstein's belief, *AJP*, 1941, 441 ff., that *relicta non bene parmula* must be a *fact*, fails because Horace has no word to show that this is

real cowardice to himself. What his allusive (and illusive) phrases obscure is obviously conduct not only better but generally known to have been better than was tactful to dwell upon. So one might disingenuously say 'Well, yes, I didn't suffer as you did: but of course I ran with the best—and my guardian angel was busy.'[1] If Horace's words mean anything, it is that he had a special and different experience from the majority, namely that he got clear of his victorious enemies on the battlefield itself. As he was able to treat with them (*venia impetrata*, says Suetonius) for a safe return to Italy more or less at once (cf. *Epi.* ii. 2. 49 f.)—with clipped wings and lowered pride, to be sure, but apparently without having to wait for the Misenum amnesty which readmitted Marcus Cicero and others—it is a reasonable presumption that it was an undefeated and undisgraced tribune, although isolated and helpless, who remained at the battle's end: *calidus iuventa* was Horace in that year.[2]

If this has been stressed at length, it is because verses 15–16 stand in strong and immediate contrast to the preceding pair. It follows therefore that Pompeius, whether he too ran or not,[3] did not likewise succeed in getting clear. Had he even managed

---

other than the celebrated lyric convention; and *non bene* is what a Roman would automatically include in that descriptive phrase.)

[1] If this sounds impossibly 'English' it may be as well to recall Büchner's observation (*Bursians Jb.* Suppl. Bd 267, 1939, 33, quoted by Wilkinson, 1) 'it is with astonishment that one notes again and again how congenial Horace's nature is to the English'. Cf. also i. 12. 37–39, where Roman greatness in *defeat* is thrice commemorated, not unlike our own attitude to Dunkirk and the Imjin River.

[2] Cf. Fraenkel, 290.

[3] It is not quite certain that Horace says he did. A feature of such descriptive passages is a transition from joint to individual action—so here *cum quo . . . diem . . . fregi . . . coronatus*; and at i. 28. 17–22 *Notus obruit* refers only to *me*, despite all that precedes of general reflection, and the *quoque*. At some point after *Philippos* such a transition may come, and it is little more than an editorial convention to put it at *relicta . . .* etc. Conversely, all the words from *tecum* to *parmula* may refer to both persons (the whole army gave way—cf. iii. 4. 26); in which case unkindness to Pompeius is only avoided if the words may be used of him, too, figuratively—that is, as a conventional attribute of a lyric poet. This is quite likely: Horace's *primus sodalium* was almost certain to have dabbled in literature, at least; and Pompeius sounds altogether like a man of letters out of his element.

to scramble away, as did so many, to the fleet at Neapolis he could have been given credit (in some cautious wording) for that. He was not killed: it remains, then, that he was taken prisoner. And as politely as he can Horace refers to this lack of resolution, prowess, and luck which made Pompeius so much more of a chattel of the victors, so to speak, and so much less able to resist absorption, like the rank and file, into Antony's army. 'You were carted (*deducte*)[1] into Brutus' battles', says Horace, 'then the tide of events, which you were of course powerless to halt, bore you back to the storms of war and exile for ten years or more.'

No ode can be dated in terms of overt reference to earlier than 30 B.C. for certain. And the degree of sophistication which (if we may anticipate our findings for a moment) ii. 7 displays in its thought-structure is hardly compatible with a composition-date before the early twenties. It is not easy, therefore, to imagine Pompeius returning to Italy before 29 B.C. It was, then, the general Augustan pardon (*victorque omnibus veniam petentibus civibus peperci*)[2] after Actium and the pacification of the East which allowed this unsuccessful warrior to come home.[3] He had known nothing from 44–29 B.C. but hardship, obscurity, and two major defeats. In view of Horace's words as interpreted here it is unlikely that he ever served, as has been suggested, with Sextus Pompeius, transferring to that allegiance with the rest of Murcus' fleet. In any case this notion would fail to explain his not returning after Naulochus and the subsequent pardon (36 or 35), even if he had somehow avoided the transfer of Sextus' legions at Messana via Lepidus to Augustus; nor will it allow for his later adherence to Antony, unless he were one of the diehard companions of Sextus on that

---

[1] Except in the (here irrelevant) use 'escort with respect', *deduco* commonly signifies that the object has no choice in the matter. It is the regular word for moving troops, parading captives (cf. i. 37. 31), and generally delivering, conducting, enticing, or driving along pupils, brides, colonists, witnesses, etc.

[2] *Res gestae div. Aug.* 3. 1.

[3] This is the conclusion of K. Meister, *EPMHNEIA, Festschrift Otto Regenbogen*, 127–34.

last ill-fated move to Asia Minor. It could be so : or it could be that he transferred to Antony before Sextus' defeat, avoiding at least one disaster, but not by being on the winning side then or later. Such action would indicate a determined anti-Caesarianism which would make even more understandable his nervousness on his final return.[1] But those who attribute this degree of 'desultatio' (*sit venia verbo*) to Pompeius (as, for instance, does Heinze) attach too much importance to the phrase *resorbens unda fretis tulit aestuosis* : the metaphor is common and easy, and Horace has no such ulterior meaning of sea-warfare when he says of himself

civilisque rudem belli tulit aestus in arma
(*Epi.* ii. 2. 47)[2]

This is corroborated by the very antithesis of the fourth stanza, for if *vv.* 15–16 are themselves to mean 'you joined Sextus Pompeius', 13–14 should convey 'I returned peacefully to Italy'—and this is going too far beyond their content. Horace does no more than indicate that he himself escaped the hot pursuit and that his friend did not.

All that can be safely deduced is that one who had no luck at or for many years after Philippi, whose appreciation of the course of the civil strife was faulty, or who perhaps had no standing or no personal tactical value to make (and carefully time) the essential transfers from losing to winning faction—that such a one, weary and disillusioned, uncertain now of his own judgement, fearful of returning at all and of the reception he may have even at the hands of his old acquaintances, must have called forth from Horace this sympathetic and careful (and almost painfully enthusiastic) poem. And from the ode to Dellius, whose complacency Horace deliberately sets out to ravage, we can gain added insight into this ode, which would not wound its recipient's feelings for a second.

---

[1] Wilkinson (33 f.) would see, perhaps rightly, in 'Iovi', 'oblivioso', covert hints to Pompeius about the new régime and exigencies of behaviour under it.

[2] Nobody will surely be so tiresome as to point out that between Athens and Philippi Horace travelled about the Aegean area in Brutus' service, obviously by sea, and suggest that this verse is meant literally.

4. *The evidence of i. 4*

The comparative approach has already demonstrated particularities of tone and feeling, and hinted at features of personal history and character, which when assimilated point to the true inwardness of the Pompeius-ode. Now that we know what Horace had to do in this ode, and have some idea of how he set about doing it, it is time to pick up an earlier suggestion and see what structure of thought may here be laid bare—and whether the structure helps the poem's function. Nobody can miss the clean break at *v.* 17—*ergo obligatam redde Iovi dapem . . .,* which sets the ode among those of uneven division of parts, here of 16 verses followed by 12, in this like the admonition to Dellius'. The likelihood is, at once, that artistically dissimilar sections here build together an erection of the type that has been called 'combined': and so it very quickly appears. And in the hope that a functional application of structure of this sort elsewhere will guide us in analysing this ode it is worth while glancing again at the way and the reason why the ode i. 4 (*Solvitur acris hiems*) emphasizes its own framework of ideas.[1] By opposing a circular motion to a linear that ode contrasts for us, perhaps just below the level of articulate consciousness, the ceaseless revolution of the seasons and the unreturning march of man to the world of death. Sixteen verses employ all possible devices to indicate their symmetry and roundness: twelve more exert themselves to drive the thought straight along. How then does ii. 7 behave in terms of progression, responsion, and the like?

A single tie, the repeated *saepe*, binds the first two stanzas together:

> O *saepe* mecum tempus in ultimum
> deducte Bruto militiae duce,
>   quis te redonavit Quiritem
>   dis patriis Italoque caelo,

---

[1] See the discussion in Chap. III, pp. 95 ff.

Pompei, meorum prime sodalium?
cum quo morantem *saepe* diem mero
    fregi coronatus nitentis
        malobathro Syrio capillos.

There are three distinguishable notions in these verses: first, the question of *vv.* 3–5, which except in so far as it may prepare the way for *Iovi* (17) is but a cry of surprised recognition and welcome;[1] then the automatic reminiscence of shared crises— relevant as placing Pompeius in his context, so to put it; and finally the more elaborate recalling of shared delights in gay surroundings—part of the essential protestation of friendly solidarity.

Then succeed these stanzas:

tecum Philippos et celerem fugam
sensi relicta non bene parmula,
    cum fracta virtus, et minaces
        turpe solum tetigere mento.

sed me per hostis Mercurius celer
denso paventem sustulit aere;
    te rursus in bellum resorbens
        unda fretis tulit aestuosis.

They are organized as a stanza-pair by maintaining in the first the idea of shared experience—even if *tecum* need convey no more than 'you were there when I did so-and-so and when the rest fared thus-and-thus'—before splitting the action in the second stanza equally between the poet and his comrade, now irrevocably parted. (A comparable construction is visible at ii. 17. 21–30—*utrumque nostrum . . . consentit astrum . . . te Iovis . . . tutela eripuit . . . me truncus . . . sustulerat, nisi . . .* etc.). The linking of these two stanzas is further achieved by the mock-derogatory expressions applied by Horace to himself in each, and by the fact that their setting is the battlefield throughout. All ideas other than that compulsive memory are discarded now and forgotten.

---

[1] Cf. *Aen.* i. 615: *quis te, nate dea, per tanta pericula casus insequitur?*—an expression, simply, of lively sympathy.

But it is essential to discern the further relationship of the two *pairs* of stanzas. The immediate cue is the *tecum* of the ninth verse, which picks up in inverted form, as it were, the *mecum* of the first. Then it dawns upon the reader that a sequence of restoration and reminiscence has given way to one of reminiscence and parting. And behind the words lie the implied movements. In the first eight verses Horace takes himself, Pompeius, and us all from the days of campaigning in 44–42 B.C. back to the earlier, carefree student days of 'pre-Brutan' Athens: then, in the second group of eight verses, the movement is forward in time, into and through the fateful second battle at Philippi itself. We are now looking beyond the mere rivets and link-devices; and it is easy now to see how the centre of the entire four-stanza sequence (i.e. *vv.* 5–14) is occupied with Horace's own history—his was the circle of friends of whom Pompeius was the chief, his the shining head at the wine-sessions, his the submission to the rigours of battle, his the encounter with the god—and only in the last distich, despite the reminders 'cum quo' and 'tecum', are we firmly led back to the standpoint of the first stanza: 'who has restored *you*, Pompeius? For *you* were last seen overwhelmed by the tide of war.' And Horace ends the first section of the ode where he began it, *in ultimo tempore*, and with no progress made at all.

This may very well be the whole point of the construction. A rounded antithetical design of this kind is the negation of progress of thought: very well, equally the mere recalling of past events, the returning of the mind to wallow in old hurts, takes a man nowhere. In his plan of thought, and (once again) not otherwise overtly, Horace poses the problem[1] and hints at a possible solution—and that is an unswerving forward movement of welcome and rehabilitation and sheer jollity. As in i. 4, the circle is succeeded by a line:[2]

---

[1] On the psychology of this ode, see Büchner's remarks in Büchner–Hofmann, *Lateinische Literatur und Sprache in der Forschung seit 1937*, 104 ff.

[2] The content of this section is 'forecast' (cf. what is said at *CP*, 1955, 166 f., on i. 4) by *mero* and *malobathro* in stanza 2, and picked up by *Massico, unguenta* in stanza 6.

ergo obligatam redde Iovi dapem
longaque fessum militia latus
   depone sub lauru mea, nec
     parce cadis tibi destinatis.

oblivioso levia Massico
ciboria exple; funde capacibus
   unguenta de conchis. quis udo
     deproperare apio coronas

curatve myrto? quem Venus arbitrum
dicet bibendi? non ego sanius
   bacchabor Edonis: recepto
     dulce mihi furere est amico.

The superficial indication of linear progress here is afforded by the shift of persons: 'redde', 'depone', 'nec parce'—these to Pompeius; then the slaves are busied—'exple', 'funde', 'quis . . . curat . . .?': then the guests are marshalled—'quem Venus arbitrum dicet bibendi?'—and finally Horace takes the floor himself, to sweep the party to success, by main force.[1] The thought and the atmosphere it conveys (and the expression which conveys both) are no longer intricate and careful, but are becoming rapidly more heated and less inhibited, more outward and less cerebral. The sentences shorten, and not only overflow the stanza but break off in mid-verse (22, 23, 25, 26, 27).[2] And this hectic career ends, for the reader if not for the partakers of the feast, with the high note (and, one might almost say, the verbal slap on the back) of *recepto dulce mihi furere est amico*!

[1] Attention is certainly redirected to Pompeius at the end (see above, p. 136), and *recepto dulce mihi furere est amico* may be said to denote Horace's conduct in his friend's presence, as *latus depone sub lauru mea* denotes Pompeius' conduct in Horace's presence. But it would be unwise to speak, on this account, of 'ring-structure' in these stanzas. *Mea* is much too weak for such a strain, and the purely attributive *recepto amico* cannot disguise the fact that the *action* passes from person to person, starting with Pompeius, and ending with Horace.

[2] Cf. iii. 25, where, in the Dionysiac ecstasy, no sentence-ending coincides with a distich-ending, and only one with a verse-ending. (Fraenkel well says (258) 'one unguarded step, and the god's ecstatic worshipper will fall down the precipice. And yet he can neither pause nor turn back'.) This is equally true in i. 18. 7–16: one might analyse that ode as a tricolon, with two verses of recommendation; four of proof; then ten of excited warning.

Of course the circle here conveys the rejected, the line the recommended course: and in many obvious ways the content of i. 4 and ii. 7 is quite unalike,[1] as is the particular function of their parts. But they are comparable and mutually explanatory precisely because they are similar essays in poetic structure; and they represent perhaps the most ambitious erections of Horace among all the architectural experiments which are one of his original and characteristic contributions to lyricism.

[1] Although one might compare their *personae*, for L. Sestius is in some ways a figure like Pompeius, having supported Brutus with loyal simple-mindedness and later returned to accept the Augustan settlement. Like Horace, however, he had avoided further quixotic conflict and won some success in peace, being chosen as suffect to Augustus in 23 B.C. (as a safe man and yet a 'republican' whose election would look well). Hence he is rewarded with a somewhat nerve-shattering, if universal, admonition: but he has not deserved the pitiless exposure accorded to a Dellius, and the words and sounds and structure of his ode form a purely artistic organization.

Index of Proper Names

Index of Horatian poems cited